BE LIKE GOD

God's To-Do List FOR KIDS

Dr. Ron Wolfson

For People of All Faiths, All Backgrounds

JEWISH LIGHTS Publishing

Woodstock, Vermont

www.jewishlights.com

Be Like God:
God's To-Do List for Kids

2012 Quality Paperback Edition, First Printing
© 2012 by Ron Wolfson

Library of Congress Cataloging-in-Publication Data
Wolfson, Ron.
  Be like God : God's to-do list for kids / Ron Wolfson.
     p. cm.
  Includes bibliographical references.
  ISBN 978-1-58023-510-5
  1. God—Juvenile literature. I. Title.
  BT107.W65 2012
  296.7—dc23
                                        2012013945

10 9 8 7 6 5 4 3 2 1

Manufactured in the United States of America
Cover and interior design: Heather Pelham
Illustration on page 9: G. Fred Pelham

Published by Jewish Lights Publishing
A Division of Longhill Partners, Inc.
Sunset Farm Offices, Route 4, P.O. Box 237
Woodstock, VT 05091
Tel: (802) 457-4000   Fax: (802) 457-4004
www.jewishlights.com

For Ellie B

Contents

Introduction

Welcome!

My name is Ron … and I have a question for you.

Have you ever made a "to-do list"?

I have.

A to-do list is a reminder of all the things we should be doing. When I write a to-do list, I take a piece of paper, or my computer, or my smartphone, and write down things I need to do.

Here's an example of one of my to-do lists:

Ron's To-Do List

Prepare for school

Go to the supermarket

Pick up the dry cleaning

Write thank-you notes for my birthday presents

Call my friend to invite him for Shabbat dinner

Read one more chapter in the book I'm reading

God has a To-Do List for you, too.

"For me?"

Yes. For you.

You are God's partner.

God needs you to continue the ongoing creation of the world.

"What? Who? Me? I am God's partner?"

Yes. You are.

Because you are made in the image of God.

It says so, right at the beginning of the Torah:

וַיִּבְרָא אֱלֹהִים אֶת־הָאָדָם בְּצַלְמוֹ בְּצֶלֶם אֱלֹהִים בָּרָא
אֹתוֹ זָכָר וּנְקֵבָה בָּרָא אֹתָם.

Va-yivra Elohim et ha-adam b'tzalmo, b'tzelem Elohim bara oto, zakhar u-n'keivah, bara otam.

And God made human beings in the image of God, male and female, God created them.

GENESIS 1:27

What do you think it means to be "made in the image of God"? Write down some ideas.

_____

_____

_____

_____

Judaism teaches that *made in the image of God* means you have a little bit of God in you.

And that God brought you into this world to do things—things that God needs you to do to make the world a better place.

These can be big things, like inventing something new. Or small things, like calling someone you love just to say "hi."

Can you think of things you can do to make the world a better place?

I'm sure you can.

This book will help you put the things you can do on a list.

Your very own God's To-Do List.

Looking in the Mirror

Find a mirror. Maybe in your bedroom or even your bathroom. Or if you are reading this in a classroom, your teacher will give you a mirror.

Look into the mirror.

What do you see?

When you get up in the morning and brush your teeth, do you look at yourself in the mirror?

What do you see?

Let me tell you what I look like in the morn-ing. I look pretty funny! My hair is usually standing straight up in a thousand directions. My face is puffy. I have that sleep stuff in the corners of my eyes. I stand there in my pajamas, looking like I should go back to bed. I haven't put on my glasses, so the image in the mirror is kind of blurry … but I know it's me.

Or is it?

Look at your reflection in a mirror. What do you see?
Write down the words that describe you.

_____

_____

_____

_____

Judaism teaches us that you are made in the image of God.

The Hebrew phrase that describes this idea is *b'tzelem Elohim* (בְּצֶלֶם אֱלֹהִים). *B'tzelem* means "in the image." A Hebrew word with same root, *tzilum,* means "photograph." When you take a photo with your cell phone or a camera, you are capturing an image, a reflection of someone or something. *Elohim* is a name of God. Every human being is made in God's image.

"But we don't know what God looks like, so how can I be a reflection of God's image?"

Ah, the Rabbis who thought up this idea did not mean that we *look* like God. They thought we should *be* like God. We should be a reflection of God's values and character.

We should act like God.

When we act like God, we become God's partner on earth—by continuing the work of creating it, repairing it, loving it.

I want you to do an experiment. Are you ready?

Look into the mirror again, right now.

"Do I have to?"

Yes. Because if you do, it could change the way you look at yourself and others forever!

Look carefully at your face.

Look into your eyes. They are the windows to your soul.

Now, look under your nose. What do you see?

A smile. Yes!

Teeth. Yes!

I once taught some students to do this experiment with their parents. Each student looked under a parent's nose. I asked the kids what they saw. One kid yelled out:

"Boogers!"

That was pretty funny!

Do you see that little mark under your nose?

It is called the philtrum. Everyone has one. Some people have really big marks. Some people have really flat marks. Even dads with moustaches have one underneath all that hair.

But where does the mark come from? How did it get there? Why is it there?

More than a thousand years ago, Rabbi Bunim, a teacher whose thoughts were included in the Talmud, asked the same questions.

With creative imagination and deep insight, Rabbi Bunim gave this explanation:

While you are still in your mother's womb, God sends an angel to sit beside you to teach everything you'll ever need to know to be God's partner on earth. Then, just before you are born, the angel taps you under the nose, forming the philtrum, the indentation that every human being has. And you forget everything the angel taught you!

BABYLONIAN TALMUD, *NIDDAH* 30B

What!!!??? You *forget* everything the angel taught you? What do you think Rabbi Bunim is trying to teach us? Write down some ideas.

_____

_____

_____

_____

_____

_____

I think Rabbi Bunim is teaching us that you … and me … and your friends … and your parents … and your teacher—*everyone* is born with the potential to be God's partner on earth, but you—and everyone—must *relearn* everything the angel taught you before you were born. That's why we come to school to study Judaism. That's why we come to the synagogue to hear God's instructions in the Torah.

When we learn about Jewish values, beliefs, and behaviors and make them part of our life, we learn how to have a life of meaning and purpose, a life that reflects the spark of God that is in each of us.

So, every time you look into a mirror and see the little mark right under your nose, remember that you not only are *touched* by an angel, but you also can *be* an angel.

How cool is that?

God Needs You

"Excuse me? Would you repeat that, please?"

God needs you.

It's true that the God of the Torah is a God who is all-powerful, all-knowing—a real miracle worker.

Yet, even God realized that the world would need a very special presence.

So God created human beings, who have the breath—the spirit—of God, to take care of creation.

God can't do it alone. That's why God created you.

"Doesn't God have angels to help out?"

Yes, but …

God doesn't depend on angels.

God depends on *you* to *be* an angel.

Has anyone ever said to you, "Be an angel"? As in: "Be an angel and clean up your room"? Or, "Be an angel and give Grandma a kiss"? Think about times when someone called you an **angel**. Write them down.

_____

_____

_____

_____

In Judaism, the Torah describes angels in heaven who help God and watch over us. Each angel is given special powers by God to carry out a particular mission. Some angels can fly; some can become invisible. These powers enable each angel to be a *malakh* (מַלְאָךְ)—a "messenger" of God. In a way, the angels were God's first superheroes!

Over the centuries, the Rabbis thought these unseen angels in heaven were not enough to make the world a better place. God needed angels on earth, human beings who can do the things that need doing right here, right now.

In a way, you are God's hands, feet, eyes, ears—and, most important, God's heart.

God needs you …

… to call someone who is lonely.

… to visit a friend who is sick.

… to read a book to your sister or brother, a friend, or an elderly neighbor.

… to make sandwiches for people who are hungry.

… to give some of your allowance to those who need it.

And when you perform these acts of kindness, no matter how small, no matter how big, you bring God's presence into the world, into *your* world. And you become one of God's angels on earth, an angel with things to do.

God has a To-Do List—for you.

Be Like God!

Has anyone ever told you to be like someone else? "I wish you kept your room neat and clean like your brother." "See how your grandma is so friendly to everyone? You can be like that, too." Have you ever wanted to be like someone else? Like a movie star, or a popular singer, or a teacher? Who would you like to be like? Write down some ideas.

_____

_____

_____

_____

The Torah teaches us to be just like someone. The Torah says:

BE LIKE GOD!

"How can I be like God?"

You can figure out what God does … and then you do it!

Just as God gave powers to the heavenly angels, God gave you talents and abilities—the powers—to make the world—your world—a better place.

Be God's Superhero

Have you ever pretended to be a superhero? Did you ever get a costume, a mask, or a cape and dress up like your favorite comic-book character? It's neat to imagine that you have superpowers, just like the superheroes.

Who are your favorite superheroes? What are their superpowers?

_____

_____

_____

Wonder Woman and Superman can fly. Mystique and Elastic Girl can transform their bodies into any shape they want. Invisible Girl can be, well, invisible. Spider-Man, the Incredible Hulk, and Thor are really strong. These superheroes use their powers to fight the bad guys, to rescue those in trouble, to defend the country, and to make the world a better place.

It is fun to pretend that you are your favorite superhero. But, remember, these characters are not real. Sure, there are times we would like to be able to fly, to be super-strong, and to become invisible … but we cannot.

We cannot be God, either. There is only One God. In the Torah, God is *The* Superhero.

However, God has given every human being the power to be God's partner on earth. We don't have to pretend to use the powers God has given us. These powers are real—and they are super!

Have you ever been afraid of the dark?

I have. When I was a little boy, my parents put a night-light in my room. When I was eight years old, I went on a Cub Scout overnight camping trip, and the counselors lit a bonfire to give us light. Even now, I keep a flashlight near my bed when I go to sleep.

Adam and Eve, the first human beings, were afraid of the dark. The midrash tells the story of how Adam and Eve were terrified the first time they saw the sun set. God sees Adam is afraid and does something incredible: God teaches Adam how to make fire so he and Eve will have light at night!

> *At the conclusion of Shabbat, the Holy One, blessed be God, inspired Adam with knowledge of a kind similar to divine knowledge ... and God took two stones and rubbed them together and made fire.*
>
> BABYLONIAN TALMUD, *PESACHIM* 54A

The rabbis who imagined this happening use the story to illustrate one of the reasons we light a candle during the Havdalah ceremony separating Shabbat from the rest of the week. It is good to have fire to light up the darkness.

But, there is an even more important lesson in this story.

My friend Dr. Gabe Goldman knows a lot about native cultures and Greek mythology. He teaches that the gods in these cultures almost never give up their knowledge to mere humans. Rather, they keep their powers to themselves. Our God, however, is different. Our God shares divine knowledge. Our God shares God's powers with us so we can make our lives better and the lives of others better. When we learn how to use God's superpowers, we become God's partners—God's superheroes—on earth.

What Does God Do?

Here's an example:

What's the very first thing God does in the Torah?

בְּרֵאשִׁית בָּרָא אֱלֹהִים אֵת הַשָּׁמַיִם וְאֵת הָאָרֶץ.

B'reisheet, bara Elohim, eit ha-shamayim, v'eit ha-aretz

When God began to create heaven and earth …

GENESIS 1:1

God creates.

Now, that's a superpower!

You are made in the image of God. God has given you the talent and ability—the *power*—to create. And when you create—you make a birthday card for your grandparent or another relative, or you bake some cookies for someone who is sick—you are doing something super. You become God's sidekick, God's partner on earth. God needs you to use your powers to continue the work of creation and to repair the world. And when you use the powers God gave you to do so, you become a real superhero!

Superpowers!

There are many stories in the Torah that teach us about God's powers—the things God does, especially together with human beings. These characteristics of God are called in Hebrew *middot* (מִדּוֹת).

Here are just a few of God's *middot:*

1. God makes clothes for Adam and Eve, the first humans, in the Garden of Eden so they won't be embarrassed.

    I'll bet if you didn't have any clothes to wear, you would be embarrassed!

2. When Adam and Eve got married, who was the wedding planner? Who did Eve's hair? God, that's who … according to the imagination of the Rabbis.

I'll bet if you have been in a wedding, you got all dressed up and had your hair done or got a haircut!

3.   When Abraham wasn't feeling well, God visited him.

I'll bet when you were sick, people visited you. Maybe they brought you treats or something to read or a stuffed animal—all to make you feel better.

4.   When Moses led the Israelites out of slavery in Egypt, they lived in the desert for forty years. What did they eat? God sent manna, a kind of food, so they wouldn't be hungry.

I'll bet when you're hungry, someone gives you food to eat. Have you ever forgotten to bring your lunch to school, and a friend shared food with you?

"Well, that's all well and good. Thank you for the Bible lesson, Ron. But what does this have to do with me?"

It has *everything* to do with you.

Because you are God's partner on earth. God wants you to use your powers.

So, just as God makes things, you are to make things.

Just as God gives, you are to give.

Just as God visits the sick, you are to visit the sick.

Just as God feeds the hungry, you are to feed the hungry.

When we imitate God's acts of goodness—God's *middot*—we join forces with God to create a better world.

It's the way we can build a relationship with God.

So use your God-given powers and do the big and little things God needs you to do.

God has a To-Do List for you.

Doing God's To-Do List

When John F. Kennedy became president of the United States in 1961, he gave one of the truly great speeches in history. He said:

And so, my fellow Americans, ask not what your country can do for you; ask what you can do for your country.

He could have stopped there, but he didn't. President Kennedy ended his speech by giving the reason to ask what you can do:

Here on earth, God's work must truly be our own.

This book is about how God's work here on earth must truly be your own. It's about asking yourself what you can do as God's partner.

Don't Read This Book—Do It!

Most books are written to be read.

This book is written to inspire you to create your own God's To-Do List.

Everyone can have one.

But everyone's personal God's To-Do List will be different.

That's OK.

If you are using this book in a class, your teacher may ask your whole group to develop a class God's To-Do List of things you can do together to make the world a better place. If you are reading this book alone or with your family or friends, each of you can make a personal God's To-Do List.

That's OK, too.

The main thing is to think about what God needs you to do … and what you *can* do … and then do it!

Here's how to do this book:

1. Read the chapters.

    There are ten chapters, and each one contains examples of one of the acts of good that God does in the Torah and some stories of how people use their powers to imitate God's ways.

2. Consider the items on God's To-Do List. At the end of each chapter, I offer ten ways to do God's work on earth. And then, at the very end of the book, I suggest three more things that should be on your personal God's To-Do List. They vary from very simple things you can do every day to big projects that could take a long time to finish. These ideas are meant to be examples for you, to get you to think about what is possible.

3. Think of what God is calling you to do.

    At the end of God's To-Do List in each chapter, there are blank spaces. Your assignment is to think about what you are good at doing—your God-given talents and skills that can be used to make a difference in the world. Think about what God might put on God's To-Do List for you. Write down a few of the To-Do's in your book.

4. Create your very own God's To-Do List.

    When you have finished the book, go back to the To-Do Lists at the end of each chapter. Pick out one or two of the things that you can do right now. Copy the page called "My God's To-Do List" on page 134. Write your name on the top. Fill it out. Put this list on your refrigerator, your bulletin board, near your bed, on your closet door, on your bathroom mirror, next to the remote control, on your computer monitor, in your smartphone—someplace where you will see the list every day.

5. Now, do your To-Do's.

6. Keep track.

When you do a To-Do, put a check mark next to the item—not to check it off, but to keep track of how you are doing, doing God's work.

7.   Think about how this is changing your life.

Once you begin to see yourself and the other human beings around you as partners with God, everything changes. You will look at the world differently. As you do, think about how your God's To-Do List is changing your relationship with God. Who knows where the journey will take you? Who knows what God will call you to do? Only you will know. Give yourself permission to grow as the godliness within you comes out.

8.   Share your God's To-Do List.

When people ask you about your God's To-Do List, tell them about it. Share your feelings about being a partner with God in making the world a better place. Work together with your class and other groups in your school or synagogue on a big "To-Do."

9.   Read your list.

Take the time to read your list. Every day. As you do God's work, recognize who you are becoming.

10.   Do one small To-Do every day.

When you do, God will smile on you. If you get stuck, read this sentence from *The Diary of Anne Frank* (Anne Frank was a teenager who hid in a secret apartment during World War II):

> *How wonderful it is that nobody need wait a single moment before beginning to improve the world.*

We Can All Be Angels—
Real Live Superheroes!

Remember, you have powers from God. And when you use those powers, you have the potential to be an angel—one of God's superheroes.

SUPERPOWER #1

Create

G od is very creative … and so are you!
Look at the very first thing God does in the Torah:

בְּרֵאשִׁית בָּרָא אֱלֹהִים אֵת הַשָּׁמַיִם וְאֵת הָאָרֶץ.

B'reisheet, bara Elohim, eit ha-shamayim, v'eit ha-aretz

When God began to create heaven and earth …

GENESIS 1:1

God creates the heavens and the earth, light, darkness, sky, earth, sun, and moon; creatures of the sea, sky, and land; and humankind.

How does God create?

With words.

וַיֹּאמֶר אֱלֹהִים יְהִי אוֹר וַיְהִי־אוֹר.

Va-yomer Elohim, y'hi or; va-y'hi or.

And God said, "Let there be light"; and there was light.

GENESIS 1:3

Then, God looks at each of these creations and thinks, "Hmmm. Do I like it?"

וַיַּרְא אֱלֹהִים אֶת־הָאוֹר כִּי־טוֹב.

Va-yar Elohim et-ha-or, ki tov.

And God saw that the light was good.

GENESIS 1:4

Then, God names the creation:

וַיִּקְרָא אֱלֹהִים לָאוֹר יוֹם.

Va-yikra Elohim la-or yom.

And God called the light day.

GENESIS 1:5

When you create something, you do the same things:

You think of what you want to create—for example, a painting. Then you get paper or canvas and paints and you create a picture. Then, you look at it. If you like it, you say, "It's good." Then, you might give your painting a name.

Think of something you created—a painting, a photograph, a dance, a song, a project for school. Write down how you did it.

_____

_____

_____

_____

Kate's Beads

Kate uses her superpower of creativity to make beaded earrings. She learned about an organization that raises money to send therapists to help children in orphanages. Kate decided to make one hundred pairs of beaded earrings to sell at a crafts fair at her synagogue and to friends and family. She raised more than $1,200—enough to cover the cost of a plane flight for a therapist to go to China. Kate picked China because her sister, Phoebe, was adopted from there. Kate is creative, just like God! Kate is one of God's superheroes.

My Dad's Toothbrush

My dad, Alan, is one of my superheroes. He is very creative. For years, he dreamed of inventing a new kind of toothbrush, one that would brush both sides of the teeth at the same time! He thought it would be great for kids. He noticed that kids can brush the front side of their teeth, but often have a hard time brushing the back side of their teeth. He tried different kinds of ideas for his toothbrush, but none of them really worked.

Then, one day, he was walking in a shopping mall and saw a custodian polishing the floor with a machine that had a large, round brush. He thought, "Wow! Most toothbrushes have brushes shaped in rectangles. What if I put two small brushes shaped into circles facing each other? Then, one brush would clean the front of the teeth, while the other brush would clean the back! You could brush both sides of the teeth at the same time!"

Dad thought it was really good. He sent drawings of his invention to the U.S. Patent Office. A patent means that you created something new. Guess what? The patent office agreed that Dad had created something entirely new and gave him U.S. Patent 346732879!

Then, Dad took his creation to an inventors' fair, and someone decided to make the toothbrush. It was called "Oralgenie." Lots and lots of kids had the toothbrush when they were growing up. Neat, huh? My dad is creative, just like God!

Moms Make Memories

Once, while shopping in an antiques store, I saw a small pillow in the shape of a heart. Stitched onto the front of the pillow were these words:

MOMS MAKE MEMORIES

I bought it immediately and gave it to my wife, Susie, as a present, for her God-given talent of creativity. Susie has blessed our family with a lifetime of precious memories. She is one of my superheroes!

Susie has been a very creative homemaker and memory maker. She makes our daily meals into experiences, our holidays into theme parties, and our big events like the Bat Mitzvah and Bar Mitzvah of our children, Havi and Michael, into wonderful celebrations.

When Havi and Michael were very young, Susie decorated our Passover seder table with frogs. Not real frogs, silly! She put plastic frogs all over the table. She placed a big toy frog at our front door; when our guests walked in, the froggy toy shouted, *"Ribbit, ribbit!"* She created a froggy centerpiece out of a green avocado. She found froggy napkins. We sang the froggy song, with lyrics written by Shirley Cohen:

> *One morning when Pharaoh awoke in his bed,*
> *There were frogs in his bed and frogs on his head.*
> *Frogs on his nose and frogs on his toes.*
> *Frogs here, frogs there, frogs were jumping everywhere!*

It was a really fun, creative seder. Best of all, our children are now adults, but they remember everything about the "Froggy Seder." You know why? Because their mom is very creative, just like God!

The Milk Carton *Gragger*

My friend Sharon is a very creative teacher. Creative teachers are superheroes, too! For Purim one year, she taught her students how to make a milk carton *gragger*, a noisemaker we use every time we hear the word *Haman* during the reading of *Megillat Esther* (the book of Esther). Sharon asked each student to bring an empty, washed-out, gallon-size plastic milk carton to school. The students each poured hundreds of dried beans into their carton and then replaced the cap. Turning the whole thing upside down, Sharon showed the class how the carton could be made to look like a head by painting a face, applying hair, and using felt pieces for a hat or a crown. Some students made milk carton Esthers; others created Mordechais. Holding the handle of the carton, the kids eagerly awaited the moment when *Haman* was chanted and shook their creations to drown out his name. Sharon is very creative, just like God!

Sharing Your Creativity

Have you ever performed in a talent show? I know a school where kids put on a great show of their creative talent. Some sing, some dance, some display artworks, some recite poems, some do tricks on bicycles and skateboards, some play instruments. Every time you use one of your God-given talents, you are being creative.

When you create, you're releasing your godliness into the world. God is the Creator.

You can be a creator, too.

Be One of God's Superheroes!

If God is creative, you can be creative. God gave you the superpower to create.

Put it on your God's To-Do List!

Create

1. Use your God-given gift of creativity—paint, draw, photograph, compose, dance, write, cook, bake.
2. Make a scrapbook to collect the memories of your "creations."
3. Make a list of your favorite songs, and ask an adult to help you create a CD or playlist of them.
4. Learn a new skill for creating, like sewing or playing a musical instrument.

5. Create some new ideas.
6. Surround yourself with creative people, creative places, and creative experiences.
7. Create a new relationship—make a friend.
8. Talk to your teacher about allowing you and your friends to create a mural for your classroom or school.
9. Ask an adult to help you plant a garden, either in the ground or in flower pots.
10. Create a diary to record your To-Do's.

SUPERPOWER #2

Bless

Has anyone ever said these words to you: "God bless you"?
People say it all the time, usually when you sneeze!

"Achoooooooooooo!"

"God bless you!"

From the very beginning, God blesses.

It's the second thing God does in the Torah.

In the creation story, God blesses three times:

1. God blesses the living creatures and birds, saying:

וַיְבָרֶךְ אֹתָם אֱלֹהִים לֵאמֹר פְּרוּ וּרְבוּ וּמִלְאוּ אֶת־
הַמַּיִם בַּיַּמִּים וְהָעוֹף יִרֶב בָּאָרֶץ.

*Va-y'varekh otam Elohim, leimor, p'ru urvu, u-milu et-ha-
mayim ba-yamim, v'ha-of yi-rev ba-aretz.*

33

And God blessed them, saying, "Be fruitful and increase, fill the waters in the seas, and let the birds increase on earth."

GENESIS 1:22

2.   God blesses human beings.

וַיְבָרֶךְ אֹתָם אֱלֹהִים וַיֹּאמֶר לָהֶם אֱלֹהִים פְּרוּ וּרְבוּ
וּמִלְאוּ אֶת־הָאָרֶץ וְכִבְשֻׁהָ.

Va-y'varekh otam, Elohim, va-yomer la-hem Elohim, p'ru urvu, u-milu et-ha-aretz, v'khivshuha.

And God blessed them and God said to them, "Be fruitful and increase, fill the earth and master it."

GENESIS 1:28

3.   God blesses Shabbat.

וַיְבָרֶךְ אֱלֹהִים אֶת־יוֹם הַשְּׁבִיעִי וַיְקַדֵּשׁ אֹתוֹ כִּי בוֹ
שָׁבַת מִכָּל־מְלַאכְתּוֹ אֲשֶׁר־בָּרָא אֱלֹהִים לַעֲשׂוֹת.

Va-y'varekh Elohim et yom ha-sh'vi-i, va-y'kadeish oto, ki vo shavat mi-kol m'lakhto asher bara Elohim la-asot.

And God blessed the seventh day and declared it holy, because on it God ceased from all the work of creation that God had done.

GENESIS 2:3

The divine blessings continue throughout the Bible. God blesses Abraham as he begins his journey. God blesses Sarah with a child. God blesses Isaac after his father dies.

Three Ways of Blessing

If God blesses, you have the power to bless, too.

You can:

1. Ask for a blessing.

    Have you ever wanted to do something and you wanted someone's blessing to do it? Maybe you asked your parents for permission to try something new. "Hey, Mom, may I jump off the high diving board?"

    Asking permission is asking for a blessing.

    Think of a time when you asked someone for a blessing to do something. Did you say "thank you" when you got the blessing?

    _____

    _____

    _____

2. Give your blessing.

    Has anyone ever asked you for something? Maybe a friend asked if she could borrow something. Maybe a new kid in the neighborhood wondered if he could join your team on the playground.

    Giving permission is giving your approval, your blessing.

Think of a time when someone asked you for something and you gave your blessing. Was it difficult to give your blessing? What did it make you think about?

_____

_____

_____

3. Count your blessings.

The third way to fill your life with blessing is to count your blessings.

When do you count your blessings? You "count" your blessings when you realize how lucky you are … to be healthy, to be in a family, to learn new things, to see beautiful sights, to enjoy all of God's creation. When you count your blessings, you use your superpower to appreciate all the good things in your life.

The Bar Mitzvah Blessing

My nephew, Avi, was born with an illness in his body, and he cannot speak. A sweet, lovable, bear hug of a boy, Avi has grown up in a loving family with his father, Doug, his mother, Sara, and his brother and sister, Aaron and Naomi. When our family received an invitation to Avi's Bar Mitzvah, we couldn't believe it! How could Avi lead the congregation in prayer? How could he chant verses from the Torah? How could he give his Bar Mitzvah speech?

When the big day arrived, the sanctuary was crowded with people. Avi strode to the pulpit in his brand-new suit and awaited instructions from his teachers.

The rabbi explained that although Avi could not speak, he would lead the service by interpreting the prayers. Before singing the prayer thanking God for the blessings of creation, Avi walked to the middle of the pulpit and proudly held up a painting he had created showing the creation of heaven and earth. Before the prayer remembering Abraham, Isaac, Jacob, Sarah, Rebecca, Rachel, and Leah, Avi held up a poster he had made of his family tree. When it came time to read from the ancient scroll of the Torah, his brother Aaron read while Avi followed along. For his Bar Mitzvah speech, Avi's mother said, "If Avi could speak, this is what he would say: 'Thank you to all of you for coming to share in my big day. Mom and Dad, sorry I got you up early this morning, but I was so excited. Aaron and Naomi, I love you, no matter what. To all my family, I keep photos of you near my bed and look at them every night. Thank you to my teachers for helping me prepare for this day. And, now remember, say "hi" to everyone like I do, hug everyone like I do, and love everyone like I do.'" Everyone was so excited for Avi! Many people were crying tears of joy.

When it came time for the parents to talk about Avi, they did not give the usual speech about how good their child was at soccer or piano playing or shopping. Doug and Sara simply stood in front of Avi that morning and blessed him. They began by using sign language to say just three words to Avi: "We love you!" Then, Doug and Sara asked God to bless their child with the traditional blessing, the same blessing offered by the high priest for the people of Israel in ancient times:

יְבָרֶכְךָ יְהוָה וְיִשְׁמְרֶךָ. יָאֵר יְהוָה פָּנָיו אֵלֶיךָ וִיחֻנֶּךָּ.
יִשָּׂא יְהוָה פָּנָיו אֵלֶיךָ וְיָשֵׂם לְךָ שָׁלוֹם.

Y'varekh'kha Adonai, v'yishm'rekha.
Ya-eir Adonai panav eilekha, vichuneka.
Yisa Adonai panav eilekha, v'yaseim l'kha shalom.

May God bless you and watch over you.

May God smile at you and offer you kindness beyond what you deserve.

May God's presence be with you always, and may you enjoy the blessings of peace.

NUMBERS 6:24–26

There is something quite amazing about this.

This is the same blessing that rabbis and cantors say at important life-cycle moments like a Bar Mitzvah and a Bat Mitzvah. If this is what rabbis and cantors say, can parents say it to their children?

In Judaism, *everyone* can give blessings.

Your parents are God's partners, and they have the power to bless you. Not just when you sneeze, but always.

That day, Avi became a real superhero. When the last prayer was recited, a miracle happened! Avi said his first word. He yelled, "Yesss!" We counted our blessings that day as Avi taught us the strength of a human soul.

Be a Blessing

In Judaism, we say and sing a lot of blessings.

Write down as many blessings as you can think of. I'll get you started:

We sing blessings over Hanukkah candles.

We sing *Ha-Motzi* before eating bread.

_____

_____

_____

Count how many blessings you wrote down.

Great!

Did you know that the Rabbis recommend we say one hundred blessings every day? We say blessings before we eat and after we eat. We say blessings when we study Torah. We say blessings when we light candles on Shabbat and holidays, when we gather together at the Passover seder, when we sit in the sukkah, when we pray.

But here's something about Judaism that is very cool.

We not only say and sing blessings, we can *be a blessing!*

"What? How can I be a blessing?"

When you do something on your God's To-Do List, you are a blessing.

When you act like an angel — a superhero — you are a blessing.

You are a blessing to those whom you help.

And you are a blessing to yourself.

"How can that be? How can you be a blessing to yourself?"

God says you can.

In fact, in the Torah, God actually calls you to be a blessing.

In the Torah portion called *Lekh L'kha*, God tells Abraham and Sarah to "go."

Go where?

God doesn't tell them where exactly they are going, but, if they go, God makes a promise—a big promise:

וַיֹּאמֶר יְהֹוָה אֶל־אַבְרָם לֶךְ־לְךָ מֵאַרְצְךָ וּמִמּוֹלַדְתְּךָ
וּמִבֵּית אָבִיךָ אֶל־הָאָרֶץ אֲשֶׁר אַרְאֶךָּ. וְאֶעֶשְׂךָ לְגוֹי
גָּדוֹל וַאֲבָרֶכְךָ וַאֲגַדְּלָה שְׁמֶךָ וֶהְיֵה בְּרָכָה.

Va-yomer Adonai el-Avram, lekh l'kha mei-artz'kha u'mi-moladt'kha u'mi-beit avikha, el-ha-aretz asher areka. V'e-eskha l'goy gadol, va-avarekh'kha; va-agadla sh'mekha, ve-h'yeih b'rakha.

And God said to Avram, "Go! Go from your land and the place you were born, from your father's house, to a land I will show you. And I will make of you a great nation, and I will bless you; I will make your name great, and you shall be a blessing."

GENESIS 12:1–2

Listen to God's call ... and be a blessing.

Be One of God's Superheroes!

If God can bless, you can bless. God gave you the superpower to bless.

You can ask for blessings, you can give your blessing, you can count your blessings, and you can be a blessing by doing God's To-Do List.

Put it on your God's To-Do List!

Bless

1. Say "God bless you," not just when someone sneezes but when someone does something wonderful.
2. Ask for your parent's or parents' blessing before you do something for the first time.
3. Bless your country, especially when you sing "God Bless America" or when you say the Pledge of Allegiance.
4. Think about the blessings in your life before you go to sleep. A famous old song (ask your grandparents or another older adult!) says, "Count your blessings instead of sheep!"
5. If someone does something really nice for you, write a thank-you note or e-mail.
6. Bless God for the food you eat; say *Ha-Motzi* before you eat and *Birkat Ha-Mazon* after you eat.
7. Learn other blessings to say during prayer services.
8. Ask your parents to give you a blessing on Shabbat and holidays.
9. Think of yourself as a blessing. You are!
10. Count your blessings. Start today. Make a list of your blessings and put it where you will see it—every day.

!

SUPERPOWER #3

Rest

After six days of creating, God does something surprising. God rests.

וַיְכֻלּוּ הַשָּׁמַיִם וְהָאָרֶץ וְכָל־צְבָאָם. וַיְכַל אֱלֹהִים בַּיּוֹם הַשְּׁבִיעִי מְלַאכְתּוֹ אֲשֶׁר עָשָׂה וַיִּשְׁבֹּת בַּיּוֹם הַשְּׁבִיעִי מִכָּל־מְלַאכְתּוֹ אֲשֶׁר עָשָׂה. וַיְבָרֶךְ אֱלֹהִים אֶת־יוֹם הַשְּׁבִיעִי וַיְקַדֵּשׁ אֹתוֹ כִּי בוֹ שָׁבַת מִכָּל־מְלַאכְתּוֹ אֲשֶׁר־בָּרָא אֱלֹהִים לַעֲשׂוֹת.

Va-y'khulu ha-shamayim v'ha-aretz, v'khol tz'va-am. Va-y'khal Elohim ba-yom ha-sh'vi-i m'lakhto asher asa, va-yishbot ba-yom ha-sh'vi-i mi-kol m'lakhto asher asa. Va-y'varekh Elohim et-yom ha-sh'vi-i, va-y'kadeish oto, ki vo shavat mi-kol m'lakhto asher bara Elohim la-asot.

43

And the heavens and the earth were completed and formed. On the seventh day God finished the work that God had been doing, and God ceased on the seventh day from all the work that God had done. And God blessed the seventh day and declared it holy, because on it God ceased from all the work that God had done.

GENESIS 2:1–3

"Wait a minute! God has to rest?"

Yep.

Everyone needs rest once in a while.

Even God.

The Hebrew word used in the Torah—*shavat* (שָׁבַת)—means "stop."

God stopped creating on the seventh day. Rest is what happens when you stop the work of creating.

The biblical notion of a Sabbath day is one of God's great gifts to humankind. It is so important that it is number four on God's Original Top Ten To-Do List (the Ten Commandments):

זָכוֹר אֶת־יוֹם הַשַּׁבָּת לְקַדְּשׁוֹ.

Zachor et-yom ha-shabbat l'kadsho.

Observe the Sabbath day and keep it holy.

EXODUS 20:8

Busy, Busy, Busy!

God was very busy creating the whole world.

You're very busy creating *your* world, too!

Make a list of all the things you do during the week: school, after-school activities, lessons, sports.

_____

_____

_____

_____

_____

_____

Take a Break

I know a ten-year-old boy, Joey, who is always tired. Who can blame him? Here's what he does all week:

Joey gets up every weekday morning at 7:00 a.m. He brushes his teeth, gets dressed, and runs downstairs to rush through breakfast. He grabs the lunchbox his mother prepares for him, and he and his sister pile into the car. They drive to two neighbor friends to pick up other kids who go to the same school. At 8:30 a.m., school begins. Joey is a good student, and there is always so much to do in class. At recess, Joey likes to go out on the playground and shoot some baskets or play dodgeball. At 3:15 p.m., school is over. One of the other carpool moms picks up

Joey and his friends, and they head home. But, every afternoon, Joey has something else to do. Twice a week, Joey goes to Hebrew school. On other afternoons, Joey has guitar lessons, soccer practice, an orthodontia appointment, or karate. After dinner, Joey does his homework and then watches television or plays video games. By Friday afternoon, Joey is so tired he can barely stay awake. The weekend is also filled with activities. It seems as if Joey never rests.

Joey needs to take time off. Joey needs Shabbat!

So do you.

Get Enough Sleep

Amy is a very active nine-year-old girl who is so excited about everything in her day, it is difficult for her to fall asleep at night. Like Joey, she has a full day at school and many after-school activities. On Monday, Amy has piano lessons. On Tuesday, she goes to Hebrew school. On Wednesday, she volunteers with her dad at a food bank. On Thursday, she has ballet. When she gets home, she does her homework, chats and texts with her friends, and watches TV. Amy doesn't go to bed early enough to get the ten to twelve hours of sleep she needs every night.

What can Amy do?

Here are some super ideas for Amy—and for you—to get to bed earlier!

1. Be sure you are ready for tomorrow, tonight! Get your backpack ready and your lunch packed the night before you need them.

2. Get a parent or another adult to help. Maybe you have too many after-school activities. Or maybe you are having trouble falling or staying asleep. Let your mom or dad or another adult know.

3. (You probably won't like this, but …) Don't have a television in your bedroom. And set a time to turn off your computer or phone, no matter what.

4. Tell your body it's time for bed. Listen to soft music, read a book, take a nice shower, snuggle up in your blankets.

5. Stick with your bedtime during school nights, especially on Sunday. If you've rested during the weekend, you'll be ready to go on Monday mornings!

Now, make a list of all the ways you rest.

_____

_____

_____

_____

T.G.F.S.

If God had to take a break from creating, shouldn't you?

God knows, you need some rest.

Rest up.

Take a day off. Shabbat is a good place to start.

T.G.F.S.—Thank God for Shabbat!

A Special Day

Karen loves Shabbat. In her family, it's a special day. Instead of the usual hurry-up dinner, Karen, her brothers Max and Sam, and her mom enjoy a leisurely meal Friday night after lighting candles and saying the blessings over wine and challah. Sometimes Karen gets to invite one of her friends for a "Shabbat sleepover." She looks forward to Saturday morning. During the week, she is not allowed to eat sugared cereals, but on Shabbat, Karen gets to pick from a whole closet full of cereals (her very favorite is Cocoa Puffs!) for breakfast before she and her family go to the synagogue for services. When Bubbie and Zaydie (Grandma and Grandpa) are in town, Zaydie likes to talk about the Torah portion of the week over lunch. Sam and Max often have friends over Saturday afternoon for a game of basketball or football. Sometimes parents are invited to play, too. In the fall, the families in the neighborhood call it the "S.F.L.," the "Shabbat Football League." In the spring, it's the "S.B.L.," the "Shabbat Basketball League." She doesn't like to admit it, but on some Saturdays late in the day, Karen will take a nap. The day ends with her favorite ceremony—Havdalah—the separation of the day of rest from the rest of the week. Her Bubbie told her to look at her fingernails in the light of the Havdalah candle to see how much they grew that week! "It's a different kind of day," Karen says. "I like it!"

Shabbat is not just a time for rest. By welcoming the Sabbath on a weekly basis, you get quality time with your family and friends. In a time when everyone is exhausted from school, homework, lessons, sports, and other activities, time off just to be together is one of the greatest gifts we can give one another.

Be One of God's Superheroes!

If God rests, you can rest. God gave you the superpower to rest.
Put it on your God's To-Do List!

Rest

1. Give yourself a break from your busy daily routine. See the next suggestion for a good place to start!
2. Celebrate Shabbat.
3. Turn off your computer and cell phone for twenty-four hours.
4. Take a walk. If you see flowers, stop and smell them.
5. Take a nap in the middle of the day on your day of rest.
6. Go to the synagogue for Shabbat services with your family or your junior congregation friends.
7. Make sure your family and friends are getting the rest they need.
8. Ask if you can invite friends over for Shabbat dinner or lunch.
9. Pray, sing, study, and rest—for a whole day!
10. Plan a vacation with your family.

SUPERPOWER #4

Call

God likes to call human beings.
    Not phone calls.
God calls.
God is calling all the time.
People call God all the time, too.
These calls are called prayer.
In the Torah, God hears and answers calls.
Do you text?
Lots of kids do.
In a way, the Torah is one big text from God.
If God makes and answers calls, shouldn't you?

Making Calls

Have you made any phone calls lately?

Look at this commandment, number five on God's Original Top Ten To-Do List:

כַּבֵּד אֶת־אָבִיךָ וְאֶת־אִמֶּךָ.

Kabeid et-avikha v'et imekha.

Honor your father and your mother.

EXODUS 20:12

When I read this, I think about grandfathers and grandmothers, too.

What does it mean to honor parents? What does it mean to honor grandparents?

At the very least, it means keeping in touch.

So, how about adding this to your God's To-Do List:

Call your grandmother! Call your grandfather! If your father or mother is out of town on business, be sure to call that parent.

In an age when many people communicate electronically via e-mail and texting, we are in danger of losing the power of the personal phone call.

My Friend Harvey

I have a wonderful friend, Harvey Bodansky, a sixty-two-year-old man who has lived with a bad disease called cerebral palsy since he was a child. Brilliant and funny, Harvey calls on people who are not disabled to help those with special needs go to college. Although his speech is difficult to understand sometimes, Harvey communicates well. We met when his father brought Harvey to a convention where I was speaking, and we became good friends.

Every year, on Harvey's birthday, I call Harvey. Every year, on my birthday, Harvey calls me. We catch up on our lives, our work, our families.

Harvey has a fantastic memory; he remembers everything I have told him over the years. To know another human being who daily overcomes enormous obstacles and yet makes significant contributions to making the world a better place is a great gift. I put Harvey's birthday on my calendar so I won't forget to call. It's a good idea to put all of your loved ones' birthdays on your calendar so you won't forget to call them or say something nice to them when you see them. Receiving a call on your birthday is one of the simplest yet most appreciated reminders that you are loved.

Who do you call? Who calls you?

_____

_____

_____

_____

_____

God Calls

The first of God's calls in the Bible is to Adam and Eve, human beings made in the divine image to be God's partners.

Here's the scene (Genesis 2:15–3:8):

God makes Adam and places him in the Garden of Eden, telling him to eat the fruit of any tree, except the Tree of Knowledge of Good and Evil.

Then, God decides it is not good for man to be alone. So God creates a woman, Eve, who has not heard the warning directly from God, but nevertheless knows that she is not to eat of the Tree of Knowledge of Good and Evil. But when confronted by a snake, who suggests that she could eat from the tree, Eve eats the fruit and Adam eats it, too. Their eyes are opened, and they see they don't have clothes on. Oops!

They hear the "sound of the Lord God moving about the Garden in the breezy time of day."

It's God calling.

In fact, the very first call from God to human beings is the very first question in the Bible:

וַיִּקְרָא יְהוָה אֱלֹהִים אֶל־הָאָדָם וַיֹּאמֶר לוֹ אַיֶּכָּה.

Va-yikra Adonai Elohim el ha-adam va-yomer lo, ayekah?

And God called to Adam and said to him, "Where are you?"

GENESIS 3:9

God is not just asking for Adam's GPS location. God is asking about their relationship. God had told Adam not to do something, but Adam did it anyway. Bad move.

Between the lines of the text, I hear a deeply disappointed God saying:

I gave you permission, my blessing, to eat anything, anything at all in this fantastic garden, except one thing. One thing! The fruit from one tree. One tree!?! And you go ahead and eat it! I'm calling you on this.

And God does call Adam on it. God calls all three of them on it—the man, the woman, and the snake. God condemns the snake to crawl on its belly and eat dirt. God makes giving birth to a child painful for the woman and makes farming backbreaking work for the man. And God throws all of them out of the Garden of Eden.

It was a bad idea to listen to God's call and then do the wrong thing.

Where Are You?

Where are you in your relationship with God?

Are you listening when God calls?

Can you hear the quiet, small voice inside your head that asks you to do the right thing?

Will you respond to God's call to be God's partner … and create your God's To-Do List?

Mom's Call

My mother, Bernice Wolfson, heard God's call to work for the blind children in the state of Nebraska in the 1950s. A friend had told her about seeing a young blind man thank a local congregational sisterhood for help in preparing a braille prayer book so he could have a Bar Mitzvah.

Her friend asked Bernice to investigate whether it would be possible to start a braille group in the synagogue. Braille is a series of raised dots on a page forming letters that blind people learn to feel; it's the way they read. Even though my mom was busy raising three boys and worked in her own business, she decided to answer the call. She asked some of her friends to join her, they taught themselves how to type braille on special braille typewriters (this was before personal computers), and Mom and her friends published the first English-Hebrew Passover Haggadah in braille.

One thing quickly led to another. Mom learned that there were eight blind kids in Omaha who needed a preschool, but no school would accept them. She knew that the synagogue preschool met on Monday, Wednesday, and Friday mornings, so she asked her rabbi whether the blind kids could come on Tuesday and Thursday to use the equipment for their own school. Done. She then thought the kids would benefit from a summer camp experience. Done.

She and her friend, Ruth Sokolof, thought the kids should have an annual Christmas party. The blind children got some money and a helper to go shopping for Christmas presents for their family members. Done.

One of the proudest days of my life was when this busy mom was honored as Omaha's Volunteer of the Year. I was ten years old and got to leave school early to attend the luncheon! How cool is that!

To this day, a foundation Mom created continues its important work in improving the lives of the blind children and adults in Nebraska. My mom was one of God's superheroes!

Stepping Up to the Plate

Pierce has played baseball since he was six years old. His parents called on him to "step up to the plate" when he came up with the idea of donating used or new baseball equipment to underfunded Little League teams. Pierce named his project Bats And Balls for Everyone—B.A.B.E. He needed storage bins, so he and his family went to a garlic factory, which contributed three bins. He cleaned out the smelly bins really well and placed them at local baseball fields. He collected more than 160 helmets and many dozens of bats, balls, gloves, and more. Pierce heard the call and used his superpowers to make a difference. Pierce is one of God's superheroes![1]

What is God calling you to do?

_____

_____

_____

_____

Hear! Here!

There are two words that sound alike, but mean two different things:

Hear means "to listen."

Here means "present."

When I was a kid, my teacher would read off the names of all the students at the beginning of class.

She looked at her list and asked, "Ronnie Wolfson?"

When I heard my name, I raised my hand and shouted, "Here!"

Sometimes, it's hard to hear.

Have you ever been on a cell phone and it's hard to hear the person calling?

A television commercial once made fun of this problem. A guy ran around trying to find a better connection, yelling, "Can you hear me now? Can you hear me now?"

Judaism teaches us to listen and to be present—to *hear* and to be *here*.

You probably know the most famous of all Jewish prayers, the *Shema*. It begins with the word *hear*:

שְׁמַע יִשְׂרָאֵל יְהוָה אֱלֹהֵינוּ יְהוָה אֶחָד.

Shema, Yisrael, Adonai Eloheinu, Adonai echad.

Hear, O Israel, the Lord our God, the Lord is One.

DEUTERONOMY 6:4

And, when you *hear* God's call, when your family, friends, and community call on you to do God's work, Judaism asks you to answer: "Here!"

When God calls, will you hear and give this answer?

הִנֵּנִי !

Hineini—"Here I am!"

Be One of God's Superheroes!

If God calls, you can call ... and be called. God gave you the superpower to call ... and to answer God's call to be God's partner on earth.

Put it on your God's To-Do List!

Call

1. Call the people you love—just to say hi.
2. Practice hearing. Listen carefully to someone else, and don't interrupt.

3. Answer text messages and e-mails from others. They are calling you.
4. Respect all questions from others, and give them an answer.
5. Answer this question regularly: *Where am I?*
6. If you feel strongly about something that should be done in your city or in the country, call your congressperson about a cause you believe in. You can even call the president of the United States to say how you feel about something. Here's the president's phone number: (202) 456-1111. Tell the president that I sent you. And, tell the president how old you are!
7. Call on your friends to join you in volunteering to do something for others.
8. Study how the people in the Torah answer God's call.
9. Listen for God's call. You'll know it when you hear it.
10. Respond to God's call. Remember, you are a superhero on a mission from God to do God's work on earth.

!

SUPERPOWER #5

Comfort

In the Torah, God makes another kind of call.
House calls.
Not too often, mind you.

But when God decides to visit, you can bet something important is about to happen.

Here is the story of one such visit to Abraham:

וַיֵּרָא אֵלָיו יְהוָה בְּאֵלֹנֵי מַמְרֵא וְהוּא יֹשֵׁב פֶּתַח־
הָאֹהֶל כְּחֹם הַיּוֹם. וַיִּשָּׂא עֵינָיו וַיַּרְא וְהִנֵּה שְׁלֹשָׁה
אֲנָשִׁים נִצָּבִים עָלָיו וַיַּרְא לִקְרָאתָם מִפֶּתַח
הָאֹהֶל וַיִּשְׁתַּחוּ אָרְצָה. וַיֹּאמַר אֲדֹנָי אִם־נָא
מָצָאתִי חֵן בְּעֵינֶיךָ אַל־נָא תַעֲבֹר מֵעַל עַבְדֶּךָ.
יֻקַּח־נָא מְעַט־מַיִם וְרַחֲצוּ רַגְלֵיכֶם וְהִשָּׁעֲנוּ תַּחַת הָעֵץ.

וָאֶקְחָה פַת־לֶחֶם וְסַעֲדוּ לִבְּכֶם אַחַר תַּעֲבֹרוּ
כִּי־עַל־כֵּן עֲבַרְתֶּם עַל־עַבְדְּכֶם וַיֹּאמְרוּ כֵּן
תַּעֲשֶׂה כַּאֲשֶׁר דִּבַּרְתָּ.

Va-yeira eilav Adonai b'eilonei Mamrei; v'hu yosheiv petach ha-ohel k'chom ha-yom. Va-yisa einav va-yar, v'hinei sh'loshah anashim nitzavim alav; va-yar, va-yaratz likratam mi-petach ha-ohel, va-yishtachu artzah. Va-yomer, adonai, im-na matzati chein b'einekha, al-na ta-avor, mei-al avdekha. Yukach na m'at mayim; v'rachatzu ragleikhem, v'hisha-anu tachat ha-eitz. V'ekchah pat-lechem v'sa-adu libkhem, achar ta-avoru—ki-al-kein avartem al-avad'khem; va-yom'ru, kein ta-aseh ka-asher dibarta.

The Lord appeared to him [Abraham] by the oak trees of Mamre; he was sitting at the entrance of the tent as the day grew hot. Looking up, he saw three men standing near him. As soon as he saw them, he ran from the entrance of the tent to greet them and, bowing to the ground, he said, "My lords, if it please you, do not go on past your servant. Let a little water be brought; bathe your feet and recline under the tree. And let me fetch a morsel of bread that you may refresh yourselves; then go on—seeing that you have come your servant's way." They replied, "Do as you have said."

GENESIS 18:1–5

The Rabbis have a great time with this story. They begin by asking: What was Abraham doing as he sat in the heat of the day at the door of his tent? The medieval teacher Rashi points out that he was healing; after all, Abraham had just had a *milah* (מִילָה)—a circumcision—at the age of ninety-nine! The very next line of the Torah says that "the

Lord appeared to him"; in other words, God was visiting the sick to offer comfort to Abraham. And yet, when the three strangers come into view, Abraham ignores his pain, interrupts his visit with God, and rushes to greet them, to offer them food and drink and rest from their journey. From this story, Judaism teaches the idea of *bikkur cholim*, visiting the sick—a very important thing to put on your God's To-Do List.

Being Sick

Have you ever been sick? Really sick? So sick you had to stay home from school? So sick you had to go to the hospital? What happened? How did you feel?

_____

_____

_____

I hope you've never been really sick. It's awful. You feel terrible. You have to miss school. You miss your friends. You can't do the things you like. You need to hear that you'll get better. You need someone to take care of you. You need support.

So when someone comes to visit you, it makes you feel better.

Judy and Her Wonder Dogs

Every week, my friend Judy Bin-Nun and her dogs—Raizel Dazzle, Ketzel Korn, and Shepzel Naches—visit sick people in hospitals. The dogs, three adorable Brussels griffons (they look like Ewoks from *Star Wars*), have been specially trained for this work. They jump into the laps of bed-ridden patients, who immediately perk up and smile as they pet and brush the animals. The dogs are especially popular with children who are in the hospital. Judy and her "Griffies" are doing God's work. Judy is one of God's superheroes!

Julia and Her Quilts

Julia learned to sew when she was eight years old. Her mom's friend is the director of an organization that supports families who have experienced violence at home, called REACH Beyond Domestic Violence (www.reachma.org). When Julia heard that REACH was opening a new shelter for children, she sewed children's quilts to donate to the children in the shelter. She used kid-friendly material to make six kid-sized quilts. The quilts not only brought comfort to the children, Julia herself finds sewing to be comforting to her own soul.[2]

When Grandma Was Sick

When her mom picked her up from school one day, nine-year-old Sarah could tell something was wrong.

"It's Grandma," her mom sighed. "She's in the hospital. She'll be OK, but right now, she's very sick."

"Can I see her?" Sarah asked.

"Yes, of course, sweetie," her mom answered. "But we have to think about how we can brighten her day. What do you think we should do?"

Sarah thought about it for a minute. She pictured her grandma in her mind and thought about the things she liked.

"Grandma really likes to read her magazines. Maybe we can get her some magazines, like *People*," Sarah suggested. "She loves her garden, so we can bring some flowers. Grandma loves flowers!"

"OK!" Sarah's mom said. "And maybe you can make her a get-well card with your arts and crafts things. She'll really love that!"

Sarah and her mom returned home to prepare everything for the visit to Grandma. Sarah took out her materials and drew a picture of herself and her grandma on the front of a card. She wrote a poem on the inside of the card and signed it: "Feel better, Grandma! Love, Sarah." She decorated the envelope with glitter and a heart stamp. Mom took her to get magazines and flowers. She was ready to go visit her grandma in the hospital.

"Oh, Sarah!" her grandma whispered when Sarah stood by the bed. Sarah was a little scared of all the noisy machines in the hospital room, but her mom said they were there to help Grandma get better. "Thank you for bringing me all these wonderful things! Come, tell me all about school today," Grandma said.

Sarah pulled up a chair to sit close to Grandma. Then Sarah told her grandma about everything—all her subjects, what she had for lunch, how her friends were doing, what she liked best about school.

When it was time to go, Sarah kissed her grandma good-bye and promised she would visit again soon.

As Sarah climbed into her mother's car, she felt really good.

"You did a big *mitzvah*, a good deed, today, Sarah," her mom said. "Visiting someone who is sick is one of the most important things you can do. I'm very proud of you!"

Have you ever visited someone who was sick? What did you bring? Do? Say?

_____

_____

_____

Sarah learned an important lesson that day. She could use her super-powers to comfort another person. Magazines, flowers, and get-well cards are all ways to cheer up someone who's not feeling well. But the most important thing is to be there, if possible. Sometimes the person is too sick for a personal visit, and you may have to call on the phone or visit on Skype or by video chat. But, if you can, go to the hospital, the house, the home for the elderly. The things you bring to cheer up the patient—flowers, balloons, magazines, books, cards—are reminders that you were there. Sarah did the right thing by sitting so her grandma could see her. Tell stories, jokes, and news of family, friends, and the world. Ask whether there is anything special you can do for the person—and then do it. Bring photos. Play the person's favorite music. Watch a television program together. Sing a song. Read aloud a book or newspaper. Hold hands. Offer a cold cloth. Massage the person's back or feet. Provide ice chips or fresh drinking water, if the medical staff says that's OK.

Don't stay too long on your visit. Sick people get tired quickly.

Before you leave, be sure to ask permission to offer words of healing. Remember, you can give blessings! If you don't know a formal blessing, you can say the Hebrew words *re'fu-ah sh'leimah*, (רְפוּאָה שְׁלֵמָה) which means "May you have a complete recovery!"

When you visit someone who is sick, you are God's messenger.

You are bringing encouragement, connection, and hope. You are comforting the ill by sharing your love.

Be present.

When you visit the sick, you bring God's presence to those who need it most.

Be One of God's Superheroes!

If God comforts, you can comfort. God gave you the superpower to comfort.

Put it on your God's To-Do List!

Comfort

● ● ● ● ● ● ● ● ● ●

1. When your friends or relatives are sick, bring them soup, tea, tissues.
2. When you visit people in the hospital, bring them something to read, a funny story, their favorite music, photos of their loved ones.
3. Let someone go in front of you in line.
4. Say a blessing; offer your prayers to God for healing.
5. When you see someone who looks sad or unwell, ask if there is anything you can do to help.
6. If a friend misses school, pick up the phone and call. Offer to bring your friend homework from class.
7. Invite your friends over for a meal.
8. Ask your parent or another adult to take you to visit a senior center or retirement community, and spend some time with people who live there who may be lonely.
9. Send get-well cards to your family and friends when they are sick.
10. Get your friends together to make a big get-well card if your teacher is ill.

SUPERPOWER #6

Care

Caring for another person is so important, but sometimes it seems that only when there is a tragedy (September 11th, Hurricane Katrina, massive earthquakes) people find the kindness—*chesed* (חֶסֶד) is the Hebrew term—that is often hidden in their souls.

The Torah has many stories about the caring and kindness of God. Just before Jacob's encounter with Esau, he thanks God:

וַיֹּאמֶר יַעֲקֹב אֱלֹהֵי אָבִי אַבְרָהָם וֵאלֹהֵי אָבִי יִצְחָק
יְהֹוָה הָאֹמֵר אֵלַי שׁוּב לְאַרְצְךָ וּלְמוֹלַדְתְּךָ וְאֵיטִיבָה
עִמָּךְ. קָטֹנְתִּי מִכֹּל הַחֲסָדִים וּמִכָּל־הָאֱמֶת אֲשֶׁר
עָשִׂיתָ אֶת־עַבְדֶּךָ:

Va-yomer Ya-akov, Elohei avi Avraham, vEilohei avi Yitzchak,
Adonai ha-omeir eilai, shuv l'artz'kha ul'moladt'kha v'eitivah

69

imakh. Katonti mi-kol ha-chasadim, u-mikol-ha-emet, asher asita et-avdekha.

And Jacob said: O God of my father Abraham and God of my father Isaac, O Lord, who said to me, "Return to your native land and I will deal generously with you!" I am unworthy of all the kindness [*ha-chasadim*] that You have always shown Your servant.

GENESIS 32:10–11

When Joseph is thrown into jail in Egypt, we are told:

וַיְהִי יְהוָה אֶת־יוֹסֵף וַיֵּט אֵלָיו חָסֶד.

Va-y'hi Adonai et Yoseif, va-yeit eilav chased.

The Lord was with Joseph: He extended kindness [*chesed*] to him.

GENESIS 39:21

When you care for someone, you are doing an act of kindness. Think of times when you have "cared" for someone and write them down.

_____

_____

_____

Caring for Kourtney

Jamey Geston was six years old when she started caring about others. Jamey thought to herself, "What can I do to bring hope and happiness to children who need help?"

While other kids were busy talking on the phone, texting, and chatting on computers, Jamey decided to use her supertalent to brighten up someone's day. She learned how to play the guitar and began writing songs. When Jamey heard about an eight-year-old girl, Kourtney Najjar, who had been in the hospital for many months, she offered to visit Kourtney to celebrate her eight-and-a-half-year birthday. Kourtney could not have a party on her actual birthday because she had just had a major operation. Kourtney's mom said it was a "special visit" and that Jamey was "really great!"

Jamey gave the gift of caring. Jamey is one of God's superheroes!

Caring for Sharks

Sophi Bromenshenkel is an eight-year-old girl from Minnesota who loves sharks. She believes they are misunderstood, and she is upset that millions of sharks are killed every year so people can make a soup from their fins. Sophi says, "Sharks only attack people by mistake; they think swimmers are seals."

To raise money for research on sharks, Sophie created a one-girl campaign, "Save Sharks with Sophi." She sells lemonade in the summer and hot chocolate in the winter, along with special shark-shaped cookies that she bakes. So far, she has collected $4,000.

Guy Harvey, a well-known artist of sea life, heard about Sophi and invited her to join him in using her creative talents by painting a beautiful work of art. The painting was sold for $7,500, and the money was donated for research on sharks at the University of Miami. Some of the money was used to place a GPS satellite tag on a shark so the scientists can track where it swims. They named the shark "Sophi"! Sophi gave the gift of caring. Sophi is one of God's superheroes!

Caring for the Environment

Zachary cares about the environment, so he reminds his family to recycle cans, glass, and bottles. He also collects food to be thrown away, for a compost heap in his backyard. Zachary learned about a project to recycle old stinky sneakers, sponsored by Nike, the famous maker of really cool shoes. He collected 150 pairs of shoes at his synagogue and his school and sent them to the Nike "Reuse-a-Shoe" program (www.nikereuseashoe.com). Nike then recycles the entire shoe: the rubber becomes a running track, the fabric is used for padding under basketball courts, and the inner sole morphs into tennis courts. Zachary gave the gift of caring. Zachary is one of God's superheroes![3]

Save a Life—Save a World

The ultimate caring is to save a life.

A remarkable saying from the Jewish tradition is this:

Whoever destroys a life, it is considered as if the person destroyed an entire world. And whoever saves a life, it is considered as if the person saved an entire world.

JERUSALEM TALMUD, *SANHEDRIN* 4:1

The Greatest Gift of All

Joanie Rosen saved a life.

Her brother's life.

Joanie is darling, caring, and quick with a word of praise and encouragement.

She has pet names for everyone in her family—newlyweds are "Ken and Barbie," a young cousin is *gute, gute, gute* ("good" in Yiddish). Joanie's home is decorated in everything red, white, and blue to celebrate America. She is just plain fun to be around.

One day, Joanie got one of those calls that everyone fears, and only a few answer.

Her brother, Gary, who had been suffering from kidney disease, was in danger of dying if a donor was not found. (Your kidneys keep your blood healthy.)

Joanie immediately volunteered to be tested to see whether she could be a match, and the test came back positive.

Joanie was elated; she wanted to give her brother the gift of life. Their father had died of kidney failure at the age of sixty-two—her brother was forty. He always said he wanted to try to stay healthy and live longer. But here he was, in danger of dying, needing the kidney that his sister was stepping up to give.

Gary didn't want her to do it, to risk her life to save his. "Pony," he said—he called her Pony because she always wore a ponytail as a little girl—"it's too dangerous."

But Joanie would have none of that.

The surgery was scheduled at a hospital in Wisconsin. Both Joanie and Gary were prepared for surgery at the same time. There they were, lying on hospital beds, brother and sister, side by side. Gary was already nearly asleep from the medicines, but she was not. She got up from her bed, walked over to Gary, took his hand, and whispered, "Gary, now you'll have the quality of life you deserve." Although Joanie thought her brother was already sleeping, he squeezed her hand as if to say "thank you."

The surgery was a complete success. Gary recovered and did get the quality of life he had not had for years. Joanie also recovered—although it took quite a while longer than expected—and to this day, she lives with one kidney.

Joanie gave the gift of caring. She is one of God's superheroes!

One Life

Why is one life so important? Can one life make a difference in the world?

When the Israelites were fleeing Pharaoh's army and found themselves facing the Reed Sea, God told Moses:

$$\text{דַּבֵּר אֶל־בְּנֵי־יִשְׂרָאֵל וְיִסָּעוּ... וְאַתָּה הָרֵם אֶת־מַטְּךָ}$$
$$\text{וּנְטֵה אֶת־יָדְךָ עַל־הַיָּם וּבְקָעֵהוּ וְיָבֹאוּ בְנֵי־יִשְׂרָאֵל}$$
$$\text{בְּתוֹךְ הַיָּם בַּיַּבָּשָׁה.}$$

Dabeir el-b'nei-Yisrael v'yisa-u. V'atah ha-reim et-mat'kha, u'n'tei et yadkha al-ha-yam u'v'ka-eihu, v'yavo-u v'nei Yisrael b'tokh ha-yam ba-yabashah.

Tell the Israelites to move forward. Hold your staff over the Sea, and it will split, and you will cross in safety.

EXODUS 14:15–16

But the people were afraid. They thought they would drown.

According to the midrash commentary, one person, Nachshon, found the courage and faith to step into the water, to take action. He waded out farther and farther, until the water came up to his nose and he could no longer breathe. Only then did the sea split.

Nachshon cared about his family and his people, and he took the first step—literally—to demonstrate how much he cared.

One life is all it takes to affect the world.

Making a Difference

Everyone wants to matter.

Everyone wants to make a difference.

You can, too.

Every day.

With simple acts of caring and kindness.

Here is a wonderful story about caring:

One day, a man was walking along a beach where hundreds and hundreds of starfish had been swept up out of the water and onto the sand. The starfish were in trouble; they could not live for very long out of the water. Suddenly, the man saw a young woman picking up stranded starfish and throwing them back in the ocean, saving them from certain death. "What are you doing?" the man asked. "There are so many starfish here. You can't possibly make a difference!" As the star thrower tossed another live starfish into the sea, she said, "Made a difference to that one!"

Every act of caring you do matters to someone or something in God's universe.

Show You Care

You can care, too.

By doing acts of goodness every day.

By making a difference to just one person.

Who knows?

Perhaps you can do something today that the world—your world—may talk about for years to come.

Be One of God's Superheroes!

If God cares, you can care. God gave you the superpower to care.

Put it on your God's To-Do List!

Care

1. Make a difference in someone's life today by simply caring: hold a door for a stranger; hug a loved one.
2. Do an act of kindness as a surprise for someone.
3. If you see a friend crying, ask your friend if she'd like to talk about the situation.
4. Make a greeting card for a friend, just to brighten his day.
5. Bring flowers to someone.
6. Bring a treat—cookies, bagels, fruit, Hershey's kisses—to share with your class. Check with your teacher first; some kids might be allergic to peanuts or other foods.
7. Ask your parent or another adult to take you to a soup kitchen to make sandwiches for the homeless.

8. Don't forget to call your grandparents or other beloved adults on their birthdays.
9. Give your loved ones a kiss "good-bye" … and a kiss "hello."
10. At the end of phone calls with loved ones and friends, be sure to tell them how much they mean to you.

SUPERPOWER #7

Repair

G od created the world, but it is not perfect.
Children go to bed hungry.
Bad people do bad things.
Nations fight with one another.
Homeless people sleep on the streets.
The world needs repair people.

At the end of every prayer service, the *Aleinu* is recited. It is a prayer that includes these words:

לְתַקֵּן עוֹלָם בְּמַלְכוּת שַׁדַּי.

L'takein olam b'malchut Shaddai.

[You are] to repair the world for the sake of bringing God's presence on earth.

The lesson is that God left work to be done to perfect the world, to repair what is broken. This repair work is called *tikkun olam* (תִּקּוּן עוֹלָם). The goal of *tikkun olam* is *shalom* (שָׁלוֹם), a Hebrew term normally translated as "peace." But it also means "wholeness."

You cannot be whole when the world is not whole.

You are called to be like God when you see a human being, made in the image of God, in desperate need. Your heart is touched. You not only feel sorry for the person in need; you feel that you can do something to help.

The Torah has many laws that reflect a deep concern for the disabled, the stranger, the widow, and the orphan:

לֹא־תְקַלֵּל חֵרֵשׁ וְלִפְנֵי עִוֵּר לֹא תִתֵּן מִכְשֹׁל.

Lo t'kaleil cheireish, v'lifnei iveir lo titein mikhshol.

Do not insult the deaf, and do not put an obstacle before the blind.

LEVITICUS 19:14

כָּל־אַלְמָנָה וְיָתוֹם לֹא תְעַנּוּן.

Kol-almanah v'yatom, lo ta-anun.

Do not take advantage of a widow or an orphan.

EXODUS 22:21

וּבְקֻצְרְכֶם אֶת־קְצִיר אַרְצְכֶם לֹא־תְכַלֶּה פְּאַת שָׂדְךָ בְּקֻצְרֶךָ וְלֶקֶט קְצִירְךָ לֹא תְלַקֵּט לֶעָנִי וְלַגֵּר תַּעֲזֹב אֹתָם.

U'v'kutzr'khem et-k'tzir artz'khem, lo t'khaleh p'at sadkha b'kutzrekha, v'leket k'tzirkha lo t'lakeit; le-ani v'lageir ta-azov otam.

When you harvest your land, do not gather the crops on the edges of the field. Leave the food for the stranger and the poor.

LEVITICUS 23:22

You are one of the people God chose to do the work of repairing the world.

How will you use your powers to repair the world?

Repair means to fix something. Have you ever fixed something that was broken? What did you have to do to make it better?

_____

_____

_____

_____

_____

_____

Four Really Great Repair People

JESSICA VALDES

Have you heard of *manna*?

Manna is the food that God sent to the Israelites when they wandered for forty years in the desert after the Exodus from Egypt.

Jessica Valdes knows about manna. She is only eight years old, but she is using her superpowers to repair the world.

When her family drove by homeless people on the street, they did what many people do: they rolled up their windows, locked their doors, and pretended they weren't there. Jessica thought, "That's not right. They don't have anything. I want to help." She asked her parents, classmates, and friends to collect small things like hotel shampoos and soaps and give them to her. Then, Jessica packed these things into what she calls "manna bags." So far, Jessica has collected more than thirteen thousand items.

Today, when Jessica's family members see a homeless person, they grab a manna bag from the car—they always have them on hand—and roll down the window to give the person a bag. (Look up "Jessica's Homeless Helpers" on Facebook.)

Jessica is a repair person—one of God's superheroes on earth!

DANNY SIEGEL

I have a friend—his name is Danny Siegel—who devotes his time and energy to repairing the world. More than thirty years ago, he created a not-for-profit fund to assist what he calls "*mitzvah* heroes." He searches the world for individuals who have dedicated their lives to serving others, people like:

- Ranya Kelly, the shoe lady of Denver, who began her work when she found five hundred pairs of brand-new shoes in a garbage bin. Today, twenty years later, she has salvaged more than $23 million in usable items to distribute to people in need.

- P. K. Beville, who founded Second Wind Dreams to make the dreams of older people come true.
- John Beltzer, who created Songs of Love, a group of musicians who compose original songs for children who are very sick.
- Jeannie Jaybush, who meets the needs of new moms and their babies at St. Joseph's Baby Corner in Seattle.
- Clara Hammer, the Chicken Lady of Jerusalem, who was so outraged at the sight of a poor woman who begged a butcher for bones to make soup that she established a Chicken Fund more than twenty years ago. Today the Chicken Fund enables more than 250 families in need to have a chicken for their Sabbath dinner every week. She was seventy-two years old when she became a repair person.

Ranya, P. K., John, Jeannie, and Clara are all God's superheroes on earth!

Danny himself is a tireless teacher of ways to repair the world. He draws inspiration from his study of Jewish texts and examples such as the Giraffe Heroes Project. Have you ever seen a giraffe? A giraffe has a very long neck. The Giraffe Heroes Project celebrates people who "stick their necks out" to make the world a better place. When he began his Ziv Tzedakah Fund in 1975, he raised $955, which he distributed to unknown *mitzvah* heroes. In 2005 alone, Danny collected and distributed nearly $2 million to dozens of projects led by extraordinary people of all religions, races, and beliefs. Today, some of his students have created the Mitzvah Heroes Fund—http://mitzvahheroesfund.org.

Danny is a repair person, too—one of God's superheroes on earth!

ANDY LIPKIS

When Andy Lipkis was a fifteen-year-old summer camper in 1973, a forest ranger told him that there was nothing that could be done about the slow death of trees in and around Los Angeles, due to the bad air that plagued the city. Andy called on his fellow campers to dig up an old parking lot and plant a meadow. He discovered that the California Department of Forestry had an extra eight thousand seedlings just sitting in a greenhouse, and he convinced department officials to turn them over to him and his friends for planting. Andy's project to "reforest" Southern California began to attract volunteers, funding, and press. He called his group TreePeople.

By 1977, TreePeople had recruited thousands of schoolchildren and adult volunteers and had planted fifty thousand trees. When Los Angeles was awarded the 1984 Summer Olympic Games, city officials worried that the city's infamous smog would hang over the event like a suffocating cloud. They proposed a twenty-year, $200 million project to plant one million trees. Andy told them that TreePeople could do the job in three years—at no cost to the city. Amazingly, four days before the lighting of the Olympic Flame, the one-millionth tree—an apricot seedling—was planted in a suburb of Los Angeles.

Today, TreePeople is recognized around the world for its educational programs, eco-tours, and ongoing work to repair the environment. More than twenty thousand people support TreePeople and participate in an impressive array of campaigns and projects. Andy Lipkis, the young camper who refused to believe nothing could be done, has consulted with the White House; written a best-selling book, *The Simple Act of Planting a Tree*, with his wife, Kate;

and visited China to share TreePeople's sustainability strategies. See www.treepeople.org to learn more.

Andy is a repair person—one of God's superheroes on earth!

MARISA WEST

Going to the high school prom is a rite of passage for every teenager. For girls especially, it is a night to dress like Cinderella at the ball. But what if a terrible storm destroys your home—and all your clothes—just before the prom?

In 2006, Marisa West, a seventeen-year-old teenager in Beltsville, Maryland, launched a project to find prom dresses to send to the victims of Hurricane Katrina in Louisiana. She talked to all her girlfriends and they began to collect dresses. When they were done, they had gathered more than one thousand prom dresses each!

One of the students who received a dress wrote this letter of thanks to Marisa:

Hi, I am a student at Cabrini High and in 11th grade. I lost everything in the storm; my home had 9 feet of water in it. I am soooo grateful that Miss West is doing this. All the students are so excited about the dresses and more than 100 are volunteering just to help. Some of the girls couldn't afford a dress, and many others were overstressed. This is really giving us a little sunshine in our lives after the storm. Thanks so much, Marisa West; words can't express how we feel. May God bless you and those who helped.

J. DANDRIDGE, NEW ORLEANS

Marisa is a repair person—one of God's superheroes on earth!

Do you know repair people? Think of people you know who work to make the world a better place. Write down their names and what they do.

_____

_____

_____

_____

Fixing the World, One To-Do at a Time

In a famous commentary on Ecclesiastes, a book of the Bible, we are warned:

> *God took the first human and, passing before all the trees of the Garden of Eden, said, "See My works, how fine and excellent they are! All that I created, I created for you. Consider that, and do not damage or destroy My world; for if you destroy it, there will be no one to set it right after you."*

ECCLESIASTES RABBAH 1, ON ECCLESIASTES 7:13

See God's works. See the trees, the sky, the earth.

See human beings, made in the image of God.

Understand that you are a partner with God.

When you fix a small piece of the broken world, you are doing God's work.

Be a repair person.

Be One of God's Superheroes!

If God repairs, you can repair. God gave you the superpower to repair.
 Put it on your God's To-Do List!

Repair

1. Be a giraffe—stick your neck out. Be a superhero—find a new way to help others in need.
2. When you brush your teeth, don't let the water run.
3. Recycle plastic bottles and aluminum cans.
4. Turn off extra lights at home.
5. Ride a bike or walk to school, if you can.
6. Donate clothes you are no longer wearing to a homeless shelter.
7. Adopt a dog or cat from an animal shelter, with permission from your parents or another adult.
8. Ask your parent or another adult to help you buy a tree to be planted in Israel.
9. Do a *mitzvah* project in your school or synagogue. Plan to share a portion of your Bar/Bat Mitzvah money with those in need.
10. If you see trash on the ground, pick it up and put it in a trash can.

Wrestle

There is one superpower that God gives you that may be surprising. You can wrestle.

You can argue.

You can struggle.

Everybody has tough times, when things don't go well or something happens that makes you sad.

Maybe another kid was teasing you.

Maybe someone you love got really sick.

Maybe you got into a fight with your brother or sister or a cousin or a friend.

Maybe you had trouble with your schoolwork.

When these things happen, you have a choice. You can let it get you down … or … you can stand up and wrestle with the problem until you solve it or, at least, find some way to live with it. Although it doesn't feel good when you are in the middle of it, wrestling with challenges in life builds character and makes you stronger.

The ability to wrestle, to fight through trouble, is a great superpower.

Wrestling with God

God doesn't mind a good fight.

In the Torah, there are two dramatic stories of human beings wrestling with God. Abraham wrestles with God during an argument. Jacob wrestles with God during a troubled night near a river.

Abraham is the first person to argue with God.

In the story of Sodom and Gomorrah, the Torah tells us that "very wicked sinners" (Genesis 13:13) lived there. God plans to destroy the cities, but Abraham worries that many innocent people will die, along with the guilty. He challenges God:

הַאַף תִּסְפֶּה צַדִּיק עִם־רָשָׁע.
אוּלַי יֵשׁ חֲמִשִּׁים צַדִּיקִם בְּתוֹךְ הָעִיר הַאַף תִּסְפֶּה
וְלֹא־תִשָּׂא לַמָּקוֹם לְמַעַן חֲמִשִּׁים הַצַּדִּיקִם אֲשֶׁר
בְּקִרְבָּהּ. חָלִלָה לְךָ מֵעֲשֹׂת כַּדָּבָר הַזֶּה.

Ha-af tispeh tzadik im-rasha?
U'lai yeish chamishim tzadikim, b'tokh ha-ir; ha-af tispeh
v'lo-tisah la-makom, l'ma-an chamishim ha-tzadikim asher
b'kirbah. Chalilah l'kha mei-asot kadavar ha-zeh.

Will You sweep away the innocent along with the guilty? What if there should be fifty innocent people within the city; will You then wipe out the place and not forgive it for the sake of the innocent fifty who are in it? Far be it from You to do such a thing.

GENESIS 18:23–25

Amazingly, God agrees with Abraham:

אִם־אֶמְצָא בִסְדֹם חֲמִשִּׁים צַדִּיקִם בְּתוֹךְ הָעִיר וְנָשָׂאתִי לְכָל־הַמָּקוֹם בַּעֲבוּרָם.

Im emtza vi-S'dom chamishim tzadikim b'tokh ha-ir, v'nasati l'khol-ha-makom, ba-avuram.

If I find within the city of Sodom fifty innocent people, I will forgive the whole place, for their sake.

GENESIS 18:26

But, Abraham is not sure there are fifty innocent people in the city. So he asks God to save the city if there are forty-five innocent people. God agrees. What if there are only forty? Abraham asks. God agrees. Thirty? Yes. Twenty? Okay.

Finally, Abraham pleads, "What if there are only ten?" God answers, "I will not destroy, for the sake of the ten."

In the end, there were not even ten innocent people in Sodom and Gomorrah, so the cities were destroyed.

This story establishes a different kind of relationship between God and God's partners in the world—you can argue with God.

Abraham Argues, Jacob Wrestles

You may remember the famous story of Jacob and his twin brother, Esau. Their father, Isaac, favored Esau. He was a strong, fierce hunter kind of guy, while Jacob was a weak momma's boy. As the older of the two brothers, Esau was supposed to get the "birthright," the right to have all the family possessions after Isaac died. But with the encouragement of his mother, Rebecca, Jacob cheated his older brother by dressing up like Esau and pretending to be him in order to get Isaac's blessing. How do you think Esau felt about that?

Fast-forward twenty years. Jacob is about to meet his brother for the first time since he cheated him. He is very nervous; he thinks Esau plans to kill him. So Jacob sends ahead presents as a peace offering. He prays to God to save him. He sends his family ahead, spending a restless, sleepless night by the banks of the Jabbok River, alone.

Suddenly, Jacob is in a struggle:

וַיֵּאָבֵק אִישׁ עִמּוֹ עַד עֲלוֹת הַשָּׁחַר.
וַיַּרְא כִּי לֹא יָכֹל לוֹ וַיִּגַּע בְּכַף־יְרֵכוֹ וַתֵּקַע
כַּף־יֶרֶךְ יַעֲקֹב בְּהֵאָבְקוֹ עִמּוֹ.

Va-yei-aveik ish imo ad alot ha-shachar. Va-yar ki lo yakhol lo, va-yiga b'khaf-y'reicho, va-teika kaf-yerekh Ya-akov b'hei-avko imo.

And a man wrestled with [Jacob] until the morning. When the man saw that he had not won, he pulled Jacob's hip out of its socket, so that his hip was strained as he wrestled with him.

GENESIS 32:25–26

Who is this mysterious "man" who wrestles with Jacob? A human being? An angel? Esau? Jacob's conscience? God?

The answer may be in what happens next:

וַיֹּאמֶר שַׁלְּחֵנִי כִּי עָלָה הַשָּׁחַר וַיֹּאמֶר לֹא אֲשַׁלֵּחֲךָ כִּי
אִם־בֵּרַכְתָּנִי. וַיֹּאמֶר אֵלָיו מַה־שְּׁמֶךָ וַיֹּאמֶר יַעֲקֹב.
וַיֹּאמֶר לֹא יַעֲקֹב יֵאָמֵר עוֹד שִׁמְךָ כִּי אִם־יִשְׂרָאֵל
כִּי־שָׂרִיתָ עִם־אֱלֹהִים וְעִם־אֲנָשִׁים וַתּוּכָל.

Va-yomer, shalcheini, ki alah ha-shachar; va-yomer, lo asha-leichakha, ki im-beirakhtani. Va-yomer ailav, mah-sh'mekha; va-yomer, Ya-akov. Va-yomer, lo Ya-akov yei-ameir od shimkha, ki im Yisra-El, ki-sarita im-Elohim v'im-anashim, va-tukhal.

Then the man said, "Let me go, for morning is breaking." But Jacob answered, "I will not let you go, unless you bless me." Said the other, "What is your name?" He replied, "Jacob." Said the other, "Your name shall no longer be Jacob, but *Yisra-El* [the one who wrestles with God], for you have wrestled with beings divine and human, and have won."

GENESIS 32:27–29

Something really important has happened in the Torah when a person's name is changed. Jacob's name in Hebrew had been *Ya-akov*—"the one who holds on to the heel" of a twin brother, Esau. Now, his name is changed to *Yisra-El*—"the one who wrestles with God."

The Jewish people are called *b'nei Yisra-El*—often translated as "the children of Israel." But what it really means is that we are the descendants of the one who wrestled with God. If our ancestor Jacob had the power to wrestle with God, you, too, have the power—the superpower—to wrestle. You can wrestle with your troubles. You can even wrestle with God!

Alex and Her Lemonade Stand

Alexandra (Alex) Scott and her family wrestled with a terrible disease. Just before her first birthday, Alex was diagnosed with a form of childhood cancer. Surgery on her spine caused her to be paralyzed below the waist. Her father, Jay, said, "We were told Alex would never walk and we would be lucky if she would be able to sit up on her own." Then, one day, her father put some vitamin E lotion on Alex's leg and noticed it twitch. Eventually, the treatments and physical therapy enabled Alex to walk again.

But Alex was still fighting the cancer. She had many special treatments to help make her well. When she felt a little better, Alex announced that she wanted to start a lemonade stand. She said, "I want to give the money to the doctors so they can come up with new cancer treatments for kids like me."

On July 4, 2002, the first Alex's Lemonade Stand opened in front of the Scott family home in Manchester, Connecticut. People heard about the lemonade stand on television and started arriving at 6:30 in the morning. By the end of the day, Alex had raised $2,000!

But Alex wasn't done. In 2004, she told her parents she wanted to raise $1 million. "I told her she couldn't raise $1 million in our front yard," her father admitted. "But Alex said other people could help. It could be done."

News of Alex's Lemonade Stand spread around the country. Alex and her parents, Jay and Liz, were invited to be on the *Today* show and other national television programs. People asked how they could help, and the family suggested that kids start a lemonade stand in Alex's name.

Hundreds of kids did just that. People were paying anywhere from $20 to hundreds of dollars for a twenty-five-cent glass of lemonade. In two weeks, Alex achieved her goal of raising $1 million to help kids with cancer!

Alex was very sick when she heard the news. She was just eight years old. She told her parents, "Next year, we have to raise a gazillion dollars." After Alex died, her parents decided to continue her work through the Alex's Lemonade Stand Foundation (www.alexslemonade.org), which encourages kids to sponsor lemonade stands and raise money for child cancer research and treatments. So far, the Alex's Lemonade Stand project has raised more than $50 million. Alex and her family faced her illness with courage and proved the saying "When life gives you lemons, make lemonade."

Alex wrestled with her illness. She was one of God's superheroes. Her parents are superheroes, too!

Wrestling with a Bully

Some kids think the way to be popular is to be really mean to other kids. They will tease, call people names, and otherwise bully others.

Why do some kids feel that they have to be bullies? The truth is that bullies need to put someone down to make themselves feel important or better. Bullies feel important and strong when they make others feel unimportant and weak.

Judaism teaches us to treat every human being as "made in the image of God." Bullies do just the opposite. Throughout Jewish history, we have stood up to bullies like the Pharaoh in Egypt or Haman in Persia. Today, with a strong army in Israel and with the freedoms enjoyed by Jews in North America, we are unafraid of bullies.

Ask for Help

Rachel, a nine-year-old girl, loved school. She loved to learn new things, she loved reading, and she loved her teachers. Rachel was smart, sweet, and always eager to answer a question. But there were a couple of girls sitting in the back of the classroom who started to tease Rachel. Every time Rachel raised her hand, one of the girls would whisper "Teacher's pet!" or "Know-it-all!" During recess, the bullying continued. "Nerd," the girls yelled at her. One of the bullies even tricked Rachel into lending her a book she was reading. "Hey, Rachel, can I see your book?" she asked. Thinking she could make friends with the bully, Rachel handed her the book. Immediately, the bully ripped several pages out of the book and tossed it back at her: "Here, bookworm, read this!"

The bullying got so bad, Rachel didn't want to go to school anymore. At first, when her mother asked her what was wrong, she said she felt sick. Finally, she told her mom the truth: "I'm afraid of those girls. They said if I told on them, they would beat me up." Rachel's mom called the principal of the school, who asked them both to come to her office. "I will not allow bullying in our school. I wish you had told me—and your mother—about this sooner so it could be stopped. I will deal with these girls. I will call their parents. And you do not have to be afraid any longer."

Rachel realized that the only way to stop bullies is to stand up to them. She was glad she had finally told her mom and the principal. They helped her get through this trouble in her life. She learned that lots of kids like her are bullied every day; she was not alone.

Rachel wrestled with a bully (not literally!). Rachel is one of God's superheroes!

Have you ever been bullied? How did you feel? What did you do?

_____

_____

_____

_____

If someone is bullying you, here are some things you can do:

- Say, "Stop it."
- Walk away. Act as if you don't care, even if you do.
- Tell your parents, your teachers, and your rabbi. They will help you figure out what to say and what to do to make the bullying stop.

There are other good ways to wrestle with bullying on the website www.stop.bullying.gov.

Wrestling with Peer Pressure

Have you ever felt as if you just had to do something you didn't want to do … because everyone else was doing it?

You feel like you have to wear a cool brand of sneakers … because everyone else is wearing them.

You feel like you have to pierce your ears … because everyone else has pierced ears.

You feel like you have to cut your hair a certain way … because everyone else has that hairstyle.

You feel like you have to bully someone being picked on … because everyone else is doing it.

These feelings come from peer pressure. A peer is someone who is in the same age group as you. Peer pressure is the influence of peers to take a certain action, adopt certain values—to do what others think you should be doing in order to be accepted.

Kids wrestle with this kind of pressure all the time. It begins when you are young and increases as you grow older. Sometimes what your friends are doing can be a positive influence, but often it is not. When do you find your own sense of style, your own set of values, your own way of being? How do you stand up to the pressure to be something or someone you are not?

Everybody wants to be liked. Everyone wants to be accepted by the group. Everybody wants to have friends.

But be on alert when you find yourself saying, "Everyone is doing it." Be honest. It's just not true. "Everyone" is not doing it; only a few kids are "doing it."

If you find yourself in a situation where your "friends" are doing things that you feel are wrong, pay attention to your own feelings and beliefs about what is right. It's not easy to say "no" to peer pressure, but you can if you have confidence in yourself. Walk away from situations that you know deep in your heart could lead to trouble.

Wrestling with Death

When the people—and pets—we love die, we wrestle with God. We wish that God had given them more days and years to be with us. We are sad, and sometimes angry, especially when someone we love dies too young or too suddenly. It is hard to understand when bad things happen to people we love.

Saying Good-Bye to Max

Debbie loved the family dog, a brown terrier named Max. When Debbie was nine years old, Max was twelve—old age for a dog. When he was younger, Max had lots of energy, jumping into Debbie's arms when she came home from school. Now, though, Max was too tired to jump much; he would still pant when Debbie came home, but he spent most of the day on his rug, sleeping.

One day, Max died. When Debbie's father told her, she cried and cried.

"Why did Max have to die?" she asked.

"Max was very old, Debbie," her father said. "He was just too weak to live longer. You know, he was even having trouble walking. I know you will miss Max very much. You loved him and he loved you."

That night, Debbie wrestled with God. She wondered why Max had to die. She was very sad.

The next day, Debbie's mom and dad talked with Debbie again. They said that it was okay to feel sad, it was okay to ask questions, and it was even okay to wonder why God would let Max die.

"Max died because he was too sick to live," Mom said. "God did not cause Max's death. God blessed us with Max in our family for twelve years."

That day, Debbie's family had a ceremony to remember Max. They looked at scrapbooks with photos of Max. They told stories about funny things Max did and trips they took together. They remembered how Max loved to stick his head out the window of the car when they went for a ride. They laughed about the times Max chased his tail until he got dizzy. They cried when they thought about how much they would miss him.

After the ceremony, Debbie said, "I will always love Max, and I will always remember him."

Has one of your pets ever died? How did you feel?
Did you wrestle with God?

_____

_____

_____

_____

_____

The biblical stories of Abraham arguing with God and Jacob wrestling with God teach us that God does not shut down our protests, our disagreements, our arguments. God created a world in which we have free will, a world that is not at all perfect, a world where natural disasters happen, a world in which living things are born … and they die. Do not be afraid to ask questions and wrestle with God when you feel angry or sad. Don't worry; God can handle it.

So can you. Trust that you can come through the many moments of wrestling—with illness, with bullying, with the death of loved ones, and more. Trust that you can have a relationship with God that will help you get through times of trouble and bring you to times of blessing. God could easily pin you in a wrestling match. But that's not the way God works. God welcomes your struggles and will stand with you, hand in hand.

Remember: God gave you the power to wrestle.

Be One of God's Superheroes!

If God wrestles, you can wrestle. God gave you the superpower to wrestle.

Put it on your God's To-Do List!

Wrestle

● ● ● ● ● ● ● ● ● ●

1. Praise God, but don't be afraid to question, too.
2. Stand up to bullies.
3. Never tease or pick on someone. Don't be a bully.
4. Find a cause where people are wrestling and work for it.
5. If someone says, "I don't believe in God," explain that he or she is wrestling with God and what that means.
6. Be a superhero and fight for the underdog.
7. When you wrestle with problems before you go to bed, remember that God will be there with you.
8. Have confidence in yourself. Say "no" to the crowd.
9. If you have a difficult wrestling match—say, with bullies or peer pressure—talk to your parents, teachers, and rabbi.
10. When life gives you lemons, make lemonade!

!

SUPERPOWER #9

Give

God gives. And God teaches how to give.

Remember Jessica's manna bags?

In the Torah, God sends manna to the Israelites so they have food to eat in the desert after the Exodus from Egypt.

Later, when the Israelites become farmers, God tells them to leave some grain in the corner of the fields for the poor.

Today, the United States alone produces enough food to feed the world. Why, then, are there still people without food?

There is no reason that anyone in the world should go hungry. Yet millions of children and adults go to bed every night with empty stomachs.

This should not be.

You can be God's partner on earth and help end the problem of hungry people in the world.

What could you do to help feed someone who is hungry?

_____

_____

_____

_____

Birthday Turkeys

Ben and Ania Bulis are really cool parents. Every night at dinner, they have a family conversation called "Roses and Thorns." Each member of their family has to talk about their favorite thing that happened during the day (rose) and the worst thing (thorn). One day, their eight-year-old daughter, Olivia, decided that one of the best things on her upcoming birthday would be for her to give away presents instead of keeping them. So, in the invitation to her birthday party, Olivia asked her friends to bring her a very special present: a turkey! After the party, Olivia, her parents, and her four-year-old brother took twelve frozen turkeys to a food pantry. The director of the food pantry said it was the best gift ever. Olivia used one of her superpowers—the ability to give—to become one of God's superheroes on earth!

God's Challah

This is one of my favorite stories, based on a classic Jewish folktale, retold beautifully by Rabbi Ed Feinstein, who is my rabbi:

Once, many years ago, in a small village, there lived two Jews. Reb Chaim was the richest man in the town, and Reb Yankel the poorest.

Every Friday evening, Reb Chaim would come to the synagogue in his fine Shabbat coat and fur hat. As the service ended, he walked up the hill to his big house. His servant met him at the door and showed him into the huge dining room, where a table fit for a king awaited him. He was served the most remarkable Shabbat meal and the sweetest, most heavenly challah. But none of it brought Reb Chaim joy. For he was alone. Reb Chaim had no family.

Reb Chaim suddenly realized what he needed—he needed to share his Shabbat feast with someone. But with whom? "Who is worthy of sharing my Shabbat feast?" he wondered. "Only God!" he decided. "Let God share my wonderful Shabbat feast." He told his baker, "Next week, I would like you to make me two extra *challot* (challahs)."

The next Shabbat, Reb Chaim entered the synagogue before anyone and walked to the Holy Ark. He stood for a moment in prayer. "Master of the Universe, each week I enjoy a magnificent Shabbat feast. This week, I want You, God, to share my feast. So I have brought you *challot*. Even You, God, have never tasted challah so good!" With that, Reb Chaim opened the Ark and tucked the *challot* behind the Torah scrolls.

Reb Yankel also went to the synagogue on Friday night, but he always arrived late and always sat in the very back. It had been a bad week, a bad month, a bad season. Each week Yankel's family had less and less to eat. And tonight he couldn't bring himself to face his children over an empty Shabbat table. So he sat in the synagogue as everyone left. When he was alone, he walked to the Holy Ark, stood a few minutes, and offered his prayer: "Master of the World, how can You make me go home to see my children hungry? Without Your help, God, I refuse to leave the synagogue!" With that, he slammed his hands on the doors of the Holy Ark. The Ark opened up, and out rolled two beautiful, golden, warm *challot.*

"It's a miracle!" screamed Reb Yankel. "Thank You, dear God, thank You!"

He ran home and placed the *challot* on the family table.

"Where did you get such rich challah?" asked his wife.

"It was a gift, a miracle of God, an answer to my prayers. Now let us eat and celebrate!"

It would be difficult to decide where there was greater joy that Friday night—in the tiny, poor home of Reb Yankel, whose children had never eaten challah so sweet, or in the big house of Reb Chaim, who ate and drank and sang his prayers with a new spirit.

So the following week, Reb Chaim again ordered his baker to make two *challot,* and again he placed them in the Holy Ark, saying, "Dear God, thank You for accepting my gifts." At the end of the service, when the synagogue was empty, Reb Yankel again humbly approached the Holy Ark. "Master of the World, I have come to give thanks for the joy You brought my family last week. Is it possible I could ask for another miracle?" And with that, he timidly opened the Ark, and out rolled two more golden *challot*!

This went on for a full month. And another. And another. Until a whole year of *challot* had gone by. Each week, Reb Chaim filled the Ark with his gifts for God. And each week, Reb Yankel accepted God's miracles. It was the greatest year in each man's life.

As the year came to an end, a terrible thing happened. The care-taker who cleaned the synagogue saw Reb Chaim, the richest man in the town, approach the Holy Ark carrying two *challot* and put them in the Ark before the service. And he saw Reb Yankel, the poorest man in town, take the *challot* from the Ark after the service. He rushed after both men and brought them back to the synagogue.

"Fools," the caretaker yelled at them. "You, Reb Chaim, do you really think that God eats your challah each week? It is this beggar who takes from you! And you, Reb Yankel, do you really believe that God hears your prayers and miraculously feeds your family? It is this rich man!" Reb Chaim and Reb Yankel felt sad as they realized there was no miracle.

Now the rabbi heard what had happened and called all three men to his study. The rabbi sat at his desk, staring into a holy book, shaking his head, and groaning in sadness. "Do you know that this miracle was planned since the creation of the world? It was God's special joy to see it renewed each week. Your hands were God's hands. How will the miracle be repaired?"

Looking at one another for the first time, Reb Chaim and Reb Yankel knew what the rabbi meant. The following Friday night, instead of opening the doors of the Ark to place his *challot* inside, Reb Chaim opened the doors of his house to the family of Reb Yankel, and they, in turn, filled his home with song and spirit.

Then the rabbi turned angrily to the caretaker. "You are a cruel and evil man. Now hear your punishment: You will leave this town tonight, and you will wander the world. And you will tell everyone you meet the story of the miracle of Reb Chaim and Reb Yankel. And when you die, your children will tell the story. And when they die, their children will tell the story. Until everyone in every corner of the world has heard the story. In that way, you, too, will repair the miracle."[4]

And now, dear reader, you, too, have heard the story.

Who will you tell?

Giving from the Heart

There is giving … and then there is giving from the heart.

The Torah understands that some people don't like to give. In fact, when it came time to count the number of people who were freed from Egypt, God tells Moses that every person over the age of twenty must give a half-shekel to be used in the building of the movable Holy Ark in the desert.

זֶה יִתְּנוּ כָּל־הָעֹבֵר עַל־הַפְּקֻדִים מַחֲצִית הַשֶּׁקֶל
בְּשֶׁקֶל הַקֹּדֶשׁ... הֶעָשִׁיר לֹא־יַרְבֶּה וְהַדַּל לֹא יַמְעִיט.

Zeh yitnu, kol ha-oveir al ha-p'kudim—machatzit ha-shekel, b'shekel ha-kodesh.… He-ashir lo yarbeh, v'hadal lo yamit.

This is what everyone who is counted shall pay: a half-shekel … the rich shall not pay more, and the poor shall not pay less …

EXODUS 30:13, 15

Yet, God also tells Moses to accept gifts …

...מֵאֵת כָּל־אִישׁ אֲשֶׁר יִדְּבֶנּוּ לִבּוֹ...

… mei-eit kol ish asher yidvenu libo …

… from every person whose heart is so moved.

EXODUS 25:2

In another instance, the call is:

קְחוּ מֵאִתְּכֶם תְּרוּמָה לַיהוָה כֹּל נְדִיב לִבּוֹ.

K'chu mei-itkhem t'rumah l'Adonai, kol n'div libo.

Take from among you gifts to the Lord, everyone whose heart is so moved.

EXODUS 35:5

How do you give from the heart?

You give happily. You give not only material gifts, but also the gift of a happy heart.

When your heart is happy, you see the other person differently. You don't see the homeless person on the street as lazy. You see a human being, made in the image of God. When you open your heart and let the love come out, you open your hand.

When you give, you take.

You take in the knowledge that your loving gift will make something good happen.

You take into your heart a sense of generosity of spirit.

When you give, your heart is filled with gratitude that your gift has made a difference.

Giving from the heart means giving with love.

Giving Your Self

Sometimes, the best gift is not money, or food, or presents.

Sometimes, the best gift to give is your self!

Johnathan Cohen loves to play the trumpet. He says it makes people happy. When he was preparing for his Bar Mitzvah at Emanuel Synagogue in West Hartford, Connecticut, his tutor, Moshe Pinchover, invited Johnathan to play in his group, the Heavy Shtetl Klezmer Band. Johnathan and the adults in the band visit the Hebrew Home and Hospital every month to perform for the people there. Even though many of them are sick, the music puts smiles on their faces as they sing and move to the music. For Johnathan, giving of his talent and his time gives him a good feeling, and he encourages others to do the same thing.

Giving of your self can be the greatest gift of all.

Have you ever given your time or talents as a present?

_____

_____

_____

_____

_____

Be a Messenger

Before our first trip to Israel, the most amazing thing happened.

I was telling a friend that my wife, Susie, and I were leaving in a week, and suddenly he pulled out his wallet, took out a $1 bill, and handed it to me.

"This is for *tzedakah* (צְדָקָה), for charity," he said. "Find someone in Israel who needs the money. Now, you are a *shaliach mitzvah* (שְׁלִיחַ מִצְוָה)—a *mitzvah* messenger. God will protect you."

I understood immediately. My trip now had an extra-special goal, a task that elevated the experience from a vacation to a journey with a sacred purpose.

I folded the dollar bill carefully and stuck it in a corner of my wallet—and in a corner of my heart. I thought about it constantly—who would I find who needed the dollar? How would it feel when I finally gave it?

On a street in Jerusalem, I saw her. She was an old woman, dressed in tattered clothes, sitting on the stone pavement in the corner of an alleyway. Her teeth had rotted away, and her hair was tangled under a worn scarf. She mumbled something in Hebrew as I approached, her hand out, an anxious look in her eyes. I took out my wallet and found the dollar bill that my friend had asked me to deliver to someone who needed the money. I handed her the dollar, and her eyes lit up. She took it quickly and put it away in her clothing. She said nothing, but I did: "*Todah,*" I whispered. "Thank you." I walked away on a cloud, grateful that my mission had been accomplished, privileged that God had watched over me and blessed me to do this good deed, this small act of kindness.

Everyone involved in that moment was doing God's work. I fulfilled the obligation to complete the task I was given. My friend, the donor of the dollar, not only performed the *mitzvah* of giving, but he also did the *mitzvah* of making my journey meaningful. And, although she didn't realize it, the poor woman had received a gift from someone she didn't know; I was only the *shaliach* (messenger). Of all the donations I have made in my life, giving that dollar bill was the most meaningful one of all.

Giving Is Life

In the Land of Israel, there are two large bodies of water. In the north, there is a large lake called the Sea of Galilee. It is teeming with fish, and people enjoy its breezes. The Jordan River feeds it in the northern end and then continues its journey to the south. There is another body of water in the southern desert called the Dead Sea. It has no life in it, it smells terrible, and no one lives around it. The Jordan River flows into it, but does not flow out.

What is the difference between these two bodies of water?

The Sea of Galilee gives and lives.

The Dead Sea gives nothing. It only takes. Just as there are two seas in Israel, so there are two kinds of people in the world.

Sir Winston Churchill said, "We make a living by what we get, we make a life by what we give."

Think of all the God-given talents and gifts you have to give.

Be One of God's Superheroes!

If God gives, you can give. God gave you the superpower to give.

Put it on your God's To-Do List!

Give

1. Think of one of your superpowers. Now use it to help others.
2. Give some of your allowance to someone who needs it.
3. Give someone a book you love.
4. Give of your time. Ask your parents, brothers and sisters, or friends to help you volunteer for a group that needs your help.

5. Give generously with a full heart.
6. Bring some cans of food to your school or synagogue before Yom Kippur to give to a community food pantry.
7. Put a *tzedakah* box next to your bed. Put some money in it as often as you can, especially before Shabbat. When it is full, open it, count the money, and decide how you will give it away.
8. Give away your old clothes or toys.
9. Surprise someone!
10. Ask your parent or another adult to help you build a lemonade stand; donate the money to a charity.

!

Forgive

It may be the two most difficult things anyone is asked to do: saying "I'm sorry" to someone when you mess up ... and saying "I forgive you" when someone says "I'm sorry" to you.

God forgives.

In the Torah, the most dramatic example of God's forgiveness is the experience at Mount Sinai. Moses has led the people of Israel out of Egypt and into the desert. There, on the mountaintop, Moses receives the Ten Commandments directly from God.

Moses spends forty days and forty nights on the mountain. Meanwhile, the people are afraid their leader has disappeared. They create an idol, a golden calf, to which they pray. God tells Moses what has happened and threatens to destroy the people.

וַיֹּאמֶר יְהֹוָה אֶל־מֹשֶׁה רָאִיתִי אֶת־הָעָם הַזֶּה וְהִנֵּה
עַם־קְשֵׁה־עֹרֶף הוּא. וְעַתָּה הַנִּיחָה לִּי וְיִחַר־אַפִּי בָהֶם
וַאֲכַלֵּם וְאֶעֱשֶׂה אוֹתְךָ לְגוֹי גָּדוֹל.

*Va-yomer Adonai el Moshe, rah'iti et-ha-am ha-zeh, v'hinei
am-k'shei-oref hu. V'ata ha-nicha li, v'yichar-api va-hem
va-akhaleim, v'e-eseh ot'kha l'goy gadol.*

The Lord said to Moses, "I see that this is a stubborn
people. Now, let Me be, that My anger may blaze forth
against them and that I may destroy them, and make of
you a great nation."

EXODUS 32:9–10

In other words, God is going to wipe out the Israelites and start all
over again with the descendants of Moses. But Moses will have none
of it. He begs God to forgive the people:

לָמָה יְהֹוָה יֶחֱרֶה אַפְּךָ בְּעַמֶּךָ, אֲשֶׁר הוֹצֵאתָ
מֵאֶרֶץ מִצְרַיִם בְּכֹת גָּרוֹל וּבְיָד חֲזָקָה.

*Lamah Adonai yechereh ap'kha b'amekha, asher hotzeita mei-
eretz mitzrayim b'khoach gadol u'v'yad chazakah.*

Let not Your anger, O Lord, blaze forth against Your people, whom You delivered from the land of Egypt with great
power and a mighty hand.

EXODUS 32:11

And so God agrees to forgive the people and gives them a second chance to receive the Torah.

If God is capable of forgiving, so are you.

Messing Up

Twelve-year-old Stephanie and nine-year-old David are sister and brother. Most of the time, they play together nicely. One day, the two kids got into a huge fight, and David hurt Stephanie. When their mom, Debbie, heard Stephanie crying, she came into the family room and asked, "What happened?"

"He hit me!" Stephanie shouted.

"She started it!" David yelled.

"David, apologize to your sister," Mom demanded.

"No!" David mumbled.

"Then, go to your room, David!" Mom said, as she led David into his bedroom. "You can come out when you're ready to say you're sorry."

David sat on his bed for an hour, thinking to himself, "Everybody is mean to me." Then he realized that he should not have hit his sister, even if she made him mad. He walked into the family room where Stephanie and Mom were playing a game.

"I'm sorry, Stephanie," David said.

"That's OK, David," Stephanie replied. "But don't do it again."

And life went on …

Let's face it, everyone messes up. Everyone says something that should not have been said. Everyone does something that shouldn't have happened.

Nobody is perfect. Nobody.

Even when we know the right thing to do, sometimes we do the wrong thing.

In Hebrew, a wrong is called *chet* (חֵטְא). Often translated as "sin," the word really means "missing the mark."

Have you ever seen an archery target? It's a big round thing with circles painted on it. The mark in the very center of the target is called the bull's-eye. You aim the arrow at the bull's-eye, but sometimes you miss.

In your life, you aim to be good. But sometimes you miss the target. People are hurt by what you said or what you did—sometimes, the people closest to you.

The question is: When you do something wrong, how can you make it right?

In Judaism, we do *teshuvah* (תְּשׁוּבָה)—we pledge to "return" to our good ways. We even have a whole ten-day High Holy Day period devoted to thinking about how we've goofed up and how we can do better next time. We say prayers to remind ourselves that we are capable of godliness.

Yet, all the prayers in the world cannot replace the one act of courage without which there is no true *teshuvah*. You must ask the person you've wronged for forgiveness.

And the one who is wronged must offer it, too.

Both of you have to make up.

It is one of the most difficult things to do on your God's To-Do List. Yet, because you are made in the image of God, you have the power—the superpower—to do it. You can ask for forgiveness. And you can forgive.

Have you ever said "I'm sorry" to someone? What happened?

_____

_____

_____

_____

_____

_____

Saying You're Sorry

Here are six ways to use your superpower of forgiveness:

1. Stop doing it. Whatever it is that you are doing or have done
    that has caused harm to another person, you've got to stop it.
    Asking for forgiveness begins with actions, not words.

2. Recognize that what you've done is wrong. You have to under-
    stand that you did something wrong and why.

3. Feel genuinely sorry for your actions. You've got to say, "I'm sorry."

4. Make good. If you said something to hurt someone's feelings,
    do everything you can to make it up to that person.

5. Tell God you goofed up. In the prayer service, there is a time to
    ask God to forgive you.

6. Ask for forgiveness. As hard as it is to do, you must go to the
    person who has been hurt by what you did or said, and ask for
    forgiveness. "Remember when I lied to you? I'm sorry I did
    that. Please forgive me." You may have to ask several times, if
    necessary. And it will probably be necessary.

This is not easy. Yet, if you truly want to ask for forgiveness from someone, doing these six steps of *teshuvah* with a sincere heart will prepare the way.

Forgiving Someone

As challenging as it is to ask for forgiveness, it is just as difficult—perhaps more difficult—to forgive.

One of your friends has messed up. She was spreading untrue gossip about you and you are hurt. You are angry. After a while, your friend wants to make up, but you are still angry. Then your friend works hard to earn your forgiveness: she stops telling lies about you, she seems genuinely upset about losing you as a friend, she says she's sorry, she admits to everyone else that she was lying about you, and she begs you to forgive her. Only when you are convinced that she is truly sorry do you agree to forgive her.

It takes personal courage to forgive someone.

The Rabbis asked, "Who is a hero?"

The answer: "Whoever makes an enemy into a friend."

Have you ever forgiven someone who asked for forgiveness? What happened?

_____

_____

_____

_____

Forgiving Yourself

Asking for forgiveness and forgiving require one crucial prerequisite: forgiving yourself.

You are not perfect. You weren't created to be perfect.

King Solomon said:

$$\text{כִּי אָדָם אֵין צַדִּיק בָּאָרֶץ אֲשֶׁר יַעֲשֶׂה־טוֹב וְלֹא יֶחֱטָא.}$$

Ki adam, ein tzadik ba-aretz asher ya-aseh-tov, v'lo yecheta.

There is no righteous person on earth who does only good and does not make mistakes.

ECCLESIASTES 7:20

It's not easy.

So, you messed up. And you've asked for forgiveness from the person you wronged. And he or she forgave you.

But, now, you can't forgive yourself. You feel guilty. You feel bad. You replay it over and over again in your head. It weighs on your heart. You cannot face yourself in the mirror.

Give yourself a break.

God knows, you must forgive yourself to move on.

Yom Kippur: The Night of Forgiveness

When I was a child, Yom Kippur was a time of mystery, honesty, and spirituality. In the synagogue of my youth, I would enter through the back lobby, which was lined with small memorial plaques with the names of loved ones who had died. Next to each name was a small lightbulb, which was usually turned on only on the anniversary of the person's death. But on Kol Nidrei night, every single lightbulb was on, creating an eerie glow that filled the synagogue with the memory of souls we loved.

To this day, I love Yom Kippur. It is my favorite holiday. There is something absolutely life-changing about the day. It is the last day of the Ten Days of Renewal, ten days that begin with Rosh Hashanah and end with Yom Kippur, ten days to think about my life and my purpose.

After you become a Bar Mitzvah or a Bat Mitzvah, Yom Kippur is a day when you don't eat or drink. It's called a "fast," even though sometimes it feels like a very slow day. We spend almost the whole day in the synagogue in study and prayer. Some people even wear canvas sneakers to synagogue because we aren't supposed to wear leather, a sign of luxury.

All of this is designed for one purpose: to think about how we behaved during the past year and how we might do better in the new year.

In Hebrew, this is called *cheshbon ha-nefesh* (חֶשְׁבּוֹן הַנֶּפֶשׁ).

When you go to a restaurant, at the end of the meal the waiter brings you a list of all the food and drink you have eaten and how much it cost. It's called the "check" in English; in Hebrew, it's called a *cheshbon*. The Hebrew word *nefesh* means "soul." So, *cheshbon ha-nefesh* means "a check for your soul." On Yom Kippur, we make a list of all the things we did in the past year to check how we're doing, to see if we need to ask for forgiveness or to forgive someone—even to forgive ourselves.

When you begin the new school year, do you get a brand-new notebook, new pencils and pens, a new backpack? Or do you start a new document or folder on your computer? How does it feel to begin again?

_____

_____

_____

_____

You are a reflection of God, and you have goodness within you. You have the superpower to forgive—not only those you have wronged but also yourself. Forgiving yourself begins with facing yourself, recognizing that you did the best you could, accepting responsibility, apologizing with sincerity, correcting what you can, crying for what you cannot, feeling the pain—and starting again.

It takes courage to ask for forgiveness.

It takes courage to forgive.

Forgive others.

Forgive yourself.

It is within you to do it.

Be One of God's Superheroes!

If God forgives, you can forgive. God gave you the superpower to forgive.

Put it on your God's To-Do List!

Forgive

1. Never go to bed angry with your loved ones. Never.
2. If someone says, "I'm sorry. Please forgive me," and the person is serious about asking for forgiveness, accept the apology.
3. Forgive someone for making you mad, even if he or she doesn't offer an apology. You'll feel better!
4. Forgive someone who disappointed you.
5. Forgive yourself. God has.
6. Think of someone you wronged. Call or meet face-to-face with that person. Say you're sorry. Ask for forgiveness.
7. Forgive your parents. They are doing the best they can.
8. Forgive your relatives—brothers, sisters, and cousins. You may not always believe this, but they really do love you.
9. Once a year, sometime between Rosh Hashanah and Yom Kippur, ask everyone you know for forgiveness. To each one, say, "If I've done anything to hurt you this past year, I'm sorry. Please forgive me."
10. Every new year, write your personal *cheshbon ha-nefesh,* a checklist for your soul. Make two lists: "Things I Did Well" and "Things I Can Do Better." Be proud of the first list; promise yourself to work on the second list.

In Conclusion: Just Do It!

I had a great time learning with you.

I hope you did, too.

Before I go, I have one last thing for you to do.

Look back at each of your ten God's To-Do Lists. If you thought of specific acts of goodness God would put on your own personal To-Do List, take the best of the To-Do's and write them in on "My God's To-Do List" on page 134. Pick at least one To-Do from each of your superpowers: Create, Bless, Rest, Call, Care, Comfort, Repair, Wrestle, Give, and Forgive. Put it someplace where you cannot miss seeing it every day. Write your name on the top line. Look at the list every day. More important, do the To-Do's on your God's To-Do List. When you do one of the acts of godliness, place a check mark next to it—not as a way to check it off your list, but as a reminder that you have the potential to be a superhero, to make a difference in the world, every day.

Everyone has gifts to give and things to do. The world will be a better place because you are in it. The question is: Are you ready to do the To-Do's on your God's To-Do List? Are you ready to be an angel, a real superhero on earth?

There is a famous story of an eighteenth-century Hasidic rabbi by the name of Zusya, who was found one day by his students, very upset.

"Rebbe," they cried, "what bothers you so? You look frightened."

"I had a vision," Zusya replied, "that when I get to heaven the angels will ask me about my life."

"But, Rebbe, you are a scholar who has taught us well. You are a modest man. What question could they ask you that frightens you so?"

Zusya looked to the heavens and said, "The angels will not ask me: 'Why were you not like Moses, who led the Israelites out of slavery and into freedom?' I am not Moses. They will not ask me: 'Why were you not like Joshua, who took the people into the Promised Land?' I am not Joshua."

"What are you worried they will ask you, then?" the students wondered.

Zusya sighed. "I'm afraid they will ask me: 'Why were you not Zusya?'"

What do you think Zusya was saying?

I think he was saying: "Was I the best person I could possibly be?"

Are you the best you you can be? Are you doing the best you can do?

_____

_____

_____

_____

Are you doing what you can to make this world, your world—your family, your class, your synagogue, your circle of friends, your city—a place filled with God's presence?

_____

_____

In God's grand design, each human being has a unique contribution to make, a special way to do God's work on earth. Each human being is a full partner with God in the ongoing work of creation. And God gave human beings superpowers to carry out that work.

It's all about doing your own personal God's To-Do list. At the end of the *Shema* prayer, the primary statement of faith of the Jewish people, this is the call from God:

$$\text{לְמַעַן תִּזְכְּרוּ וַעֲשִׂיתֶם אֶת־כָּל־מִצְוֹתָי וִהְיִיתֶם קְדֹשִׁים לֵאלֹהֵיכֶם.}$$

L'ma-an tizk'ru va-asitem et-kol-mitzvotai, vih'yitem k'doshim lei-loheikhem.

Then you will be reminded to observe all My To-Do's [*mitzvot*] and to be holy to your God.

NUMBERS 15:40

Just do it!

!

Three More Ways to Be a Superhero and Do God's Work on Earth

כַּמַּיִם הַפָּנִים לַפָּנִים כֵּן לֵב־הָאָדָם לָאָדָם.

Ka-mayim ha-panim la-panim, kein leiv-ha-adam la-adam.

Just as face answers face in a reflection in water, so should one person's heart answer another's.

PROVERBS 27:19

Martin Buber, a great twentieth-century teacher, taught that all life is about meeting between people.

God is not found in the Holy Ark.

God is not found in the heavens.

God is found in relationship between human beings.

God never intended for humans to be alone.

You are not alone.

You are surrounded by other human beings—made in the image of God—who have the same potential and superpowers as you to be God's partners, to live their purpose, to do God's work, to be God's superheroes on earth.

But you need to remind them. So …

Don't walk on by when you see another person who needs help.

Remember, God has given you superpowers to make a difference in the world.

Remember, when you use your superpowers, you not only become one of God's superheroes, you become one of God's angels on earth.

Remember the philtrum—that little indentation under everyone's nose. We were all once touched by an angel; we all have the ability to be an angel.

Don't give a cold shoulder. Offer a warm heart.

Share this book with your parents, your grandparents, your family.

Share your new understanding of our purpose.

Welcome someone to the partnership with God.

Encourage your friends and relatives to be superheroes, just like you!

Begin with these final three To-Do's:

1. Look at every human being you meet
    Face-to-face
    Eye-to-eye
    Heart-to-heart

2. Recognize that everyone is made in the image of God, and …

3. Smile!

!

Welcome, Superhero Angels!

One of my favorite songs is a song you may know. It's a song about what you become when you decide to be like God. We sing it on Friday night around the Shabbat table and in the synagogue.

The song is called "*Shalom Aleichem.*" It's about welcoming the superhero angels who come into our lives, especially on Shabbat.

There are four parts to the song.

Here are the words. Almost all the words in all four parts are the same. See if you can figure out which words are different!

PART 1

Shalom aleikhem	Peace be to you	שָׁלוֹם עֲלֵיכֶם
Malakhei hashareit	angels who help	מַלְאֲכֵי הַשָּׁרֵת
Malakhei Elyon	angels of the Most High	מַלְאֲכֵי עֶלְיוֹן
Mimelekh	from the Ruler,	מִמֶּלֶךְ
Malkhei ham'lakhim	the Ruler of rulers	מַלְכֵי הַמְּלָכִים
Hakadosh barukh hu.	the Holy One, praised is God.	הַקָּדוֹשׁ בָּרוּךְ הוּא

PART 2

Bo-akhem l'shalom	Come in peace	בּוֹאֲכֶם לְשָׁלוֹם
Malakhei hashalom	angels of peace	מַלְאֲכֵי הַשָּׁלוֹם

Malakhei Elyon	angels of the Most High	מַלְאֲכֵי עֶלְיוֹן
Mimelekh	from the Ruler,	מִמֶּלֶךְ
Malkhei ham'lakhim	the Ruler of rulers	מַלְכֵי הַמְּלָכִים
Hakadosh barukh hu.	the Holy One, praised is God.	הַקָּדוֹשׁ בָּרוּךְ הוּא

PART 3

Bar'khuni l'shalom	Bless me with peace	בָּרְכוּנִי לְשָׁלוֹם
Malakhei hashalom	angels of peace	מַלְאֲכֵי הַשָּׁלוֹם
Malakhei Elyon	angels of the Most High	מַלְאֲכֵי עֶלְיוֹן
Mimelekh	from the Ruler,	מִמֶּלֶךְ
Malkhei ham'lakhim	the Ruler of rulers	מַלְכֵי הַמְּלָכִים
Hakadosh barukh hu.	the Holy One, praised is God.	הַקָּדוֹשׁ בָּרוּךְ הוּא

PART 4

Tzeit'khem l'shalom	Go in peace	צֵאתְכֶם לְשָׁלוֹם
Malakhei hashalom	angels of peace	מַלְאֲכֵי הַשָּׁלוֹם
Malakhei Elyon	angels of the Most High	מַלְאֲכֵי עֶלְיוֹן
Mimelekh	from the Ruler,	מִמֶּלֶךְ
Malkhei ham'lakhim	the Ruler of rulers	מַלְכֵי הַמְּלָכִים
Hakadosh barukh hu.	the Holy One, praised is God.	הַקָּדוֹשׁ בָּרוּךְ הוּא

Did you notice the first words of each part are different: *shalom aleikhem*—peace be to you; *bo-akhem*—come in; *bar'khuni*—bless me; *tzeit'khem*—go. We welcome the superhero angels, we invite them in, we ask for their blessing, and we send them back into the world to be a blessing to others.

There is one more word that is different. Do you see it? Look again at the second line of Part 2, Part 3, and Part 4. In each of these three parts, the second line is the same: *malakhei hashalom*; the superhero angels are called "angels of peace."

Now look at the second line in Part 1. The words describing the superhero angels are different: *malakhei hashareit*. They are called "angels who help." Another translation is "angels who serve." The superhero angels we welcome are angels who help God by doing God's work.

When you decide to be like God, when you do the To-Do's on your God's To-Do List, you become a "superhero angel who helps," a "superhero angel who serves," God's partner on earth, a real superhero.

This is my prayer for you. I welcome you as one of God's superhero angels, a superhero who is dedicated to doing God's work. I encourage you to see every To-Do that you do as a blessing—to others and to God. Never forget: You matter. You can make a difference. You are a blessing!

So sing the song! Sing it with your class. Sing it with your family. Sing it to yourself.

Welcome! You are God's newest superhero!

God bless you!

—Ron

!

My God's To-Do List

NAME_____

MY TO-DO'S

1._____

2._____

3._____

4._____

5._____

6._____

7._____

8._____

9._____

10._____

Notes

1. Adapted from Liz Suneby and Diane Heiman, *The Mitzvah Project Book: Making Mitzvah Part of Your Bar/Bat Mitzvah ... and Your Life* (Woodstock, Vt.: Jewish Lights Publishing, 2011), 111.

2. Adapted from Liz Suneby and Diane Heiman, *The Mitzvah Project Book: Making Mitzvah Part of Your Bar/Bat Mitzvah ... and Your Life* (Woodstock, Vt.: Jewish Lights Publishing, 2011), 10–11.

3. Adapted from Liz Suneby and Diane Heiman, *The Mitzvah Project Book: Making Mitzvah Part of Your Bar/Bat Mitzvah ... and Your Life* (Woodstock, Vt.: Jewish Lights Publishing, 2011), 120.

4. Adapted from Dr. Ron Wolfson, *God's To-Do List: 103 Ways to Be an Angel and Do God's Work on Earth* (Woodstock, Vt.: Jewish Lights Publishing, 2007), 91–93.

Suggestions for Further Reading

Adelman, Penina, Ali Feldman, and Shulamit Reinharz. *The JGirls Guide: The Young Jewish Woman's Handbook for Coming of Age.* Woodstock, Vt.: Jewish Lights Publishing, 2005.

Feinstein, Edward. *Tough Questions Jews Ask,* 2nd ed. Woodstock, Vt.: Jewish Lights Publishing, 2011.

Kaufman, Gershen, Lev Raphael, and Pamela Espeland. *Stick Up for Yourself: Every Kid's Guide to Personal Power and Positive Self-Esteem.* Minneapolis: Free Spirit Publishing, 1999.

Kripke, Dorothy K. *Let's Talk about God.* Los Angeles, Calif.: Torah Aura Productions, 2003.

Kushner, Lawrence, and Gary Schmidt. *In God's Hands.* Woodstock, Vt.: Jewish Lights Publishing, 2005.

Lipkis, Andy and Katie. *The Simple Act of Planting a Tree: A Citizen Forester's Guide to Healing Your Neighborhood, Your City and Your World.* Los Angeles: J. P. Tarcher, 1990.

Salkin, Jeffrey K. *For Kids—Putting God on Your Guest List: How to Claim the Spiritual Meaning of Your Bar or Bat Mitzvah,* 2nd ed. Woodstock, Vt.: Jewish Lights Publishing, 2007.

Scott, Alex. *Alex and the Amazing Lemonade Stand*. Wynnewood, Pa.: Paje Publishing Company, 2004.

Sidman, Joyce. *This Is Just to Say: Poems of Apology and Forgiveness*. Boston: Houghton Mifflin, 2007.

Siegel, Danny, and Naomi Eisenberger. *Mitzvah Magic: What Kids Can Do to Change the World*. Minneapolis: Kar-Ben Publishing, 2002.

Suneby, Liz, and Diane Heiman. *The Mitzvah Project Book: Making Mitzvah Part of Your Bar/Bat Mitzvah … and Your Life*. Woodstock, Vt.: Jewish Lights Publishing, 2011.

Acknowledgments

For the wonderful people at Jewish Lights Publishing: Stuart M. Matlins, publisher and editor in chief, and Emily Wichland, vice president of Editorial & Production, for suggesting the project; content editor Bryna Fischer for helpful editing; book and cover designer Heather Pelham for the terrific cover and interior design; and illustrator G. Fred Pelham—many thanks. For those who share their stories in the book—my gratitude.

For my inspirational superheroes: Susie, Michael, Havi, Dave, Ellie Brooklyn, and Alta Zadie Alan—when I count my blessings, you are at the top of the list!

My Notes

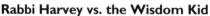

Children's Books by Sandy Eisenberg Sasso

The Shema in the Mezuzah: Listening to Each Other
By Sandy Eisenberg Sasso; Full-color Illus. by Joani Keller Rothenberg
This playful yet profound story of conflict and compromise introduces children
ages 3 to 6 to the words of the *Shema* and the custom of putting up the mezuzah.
9 x 12, 32 pp, Full-color illus., HC, 978-1-58023-506-8 **$18.99**

Adam & Eve's First Sunset: God's New Day
Explores fear and hope, faith and gratitude in ways that will delight kids and
adults—inspiring us to bless each of God's days and nights.
9 x 12, 32 pp, Full-color illus., HC, 978-1-58023-177-0 **$17.95** *For ages 4 & up*
Also Available as a Board Book: **Adam and Eve's New Day**
 5 x 5, 24 pp, Full-color illus., Board Book, 978-1-59473-205-8 **$7.99** *For ages 0–4*
 (A book from SkyLight Paths, Jewish Lights' sister imprint)

But God Remembered: Stories of Women from Creation to the
Promised Land   Four different stories of women—Lilith, Serach, Bityah and
the Daughters of Z—teach us important values through their faith and actions.
9 x 12, 32 pp, Full-color illus., Quality PB, 978-1-58023-372-9 **$8.99** *For ages 8 & up*

For Heaven's Sake
Heaven is often found where you least expect it.
9 x 12, 32 pp, Full-color illus., HC, 978-1-58023-054-4 **$16.95** *For ages 4 & up*

God in Between
If you wanted to find God, where would you look? This magical, mythical tale
teaches that God can be found where we are: within all of us and the relationships
between us. 9 x 12, 32 pp, Full-color illus., HC, 978-1-879045-86-6 **$16.95** *For ages 4 & up*

God Said Amen
An inspiring story about hearing the answers to our prayers.
9 x 12, 32 pp, Full-color illus., HC, 978-1-58023-080-3 **$16.95** *For ages 4 & up*

God's Paintbrush: Special 10th Anniversary Edition
Wonderfully interactive, invites children of all faiths and backgrounds to encounter God
through moments in their own lives. Provides questions adult and child can explore
together. 11 x 8½, 32 pp, Full-color illus., HC, 978-1-58023-195-4 **$17.95** *For ages 4 & up*
Also Available as a Board Book: **I Am God's Paintbrush**
 5 x 5, 24 pp, Full-color illus., Board Book, 978-1-59473-265-2 **$7.99** *For ages 0–4*
 (A book from SkyLight Paths, Jewish Lights' sister imprint)
Also Available: **God's Paintbrush Teacher's Guide**
 8½ x 11, 32 pp, PB, 978-1-879045-57-6 **$8.95**
God's Paintbrush Celebration Kit
A Spiritual Activity Kit for Teachers and Students of All Faiths, All Backgrounds
 9½ x 12, 40 Full-color Activity Sheets & Teacher Folder w/ complete instructions
 HC, 978-1-58023-050-6 **$21.95**
 8-Student Activity Sheet Pack (40 sheets/5 sessions), 978-1-58023-058-2 **$19.95**

In God's Name
Like an ancient myth in its poetic text and vibrant illustrations, this award-
winning modern fable about the search for God's name celebrates the diversity
and, at the same time, the unity of all people.
9 x 12, 32 pp, Full-color illus., HC, 978-1-879045-26-2 **$16.99** *For ages 4 & up*
Also Available as a Board Book: **What Is God's Name?**
 5 x 5, 24 pp, Full-color illus., Board Book, 978-1-893361-10-2 **$7.99** *For ages 0–4*
 (A book from SkyLight Paths, Jewish Lights' sister imprint)
Also Available in Spanish: **El nombre de Dios**
 9 x 12, 32 pp, Full-color illus., HC, 978-1-893361-63-8 **$16.95** *For ages 4 & up*

Noah's Wife: The Story of Naamah
9 x 12, 32 pp, Full-color illus., HC, 978-1-58023-134-3 **$16.95** *For ages 4 & up*
Also Available as a Board Book: **Naamah, Noah's Wife**
 5 x 5, 24 pp, Full-color illus., Board Book, 978-1-893361-56-0 **$7.95** *For ages 0–4*
 (A book from SkyLight Paths, Jewish Lights' sister imprint)

Children's Books

Around the World in One Shabbat
Jewish People Celebrate the Sabbath Together
By Durga Yael Bernhard
Takes your child on a colorful adventure to share the many ways Jewish people celebrate Shabbat around the world.
11 x 8½, 32 pp, Full-color illus., HC, 978-1-58023-433-7 **$18.99** *For ages 3–6*

It's a ... It's a ... It's a Mitzvah
By Liz Suneby and Diane Heiman; Full-color Illus. by Laurel Molk
Join Mitzvah Meerkat and friends as they introduce children to the everyday kindnesses that mark the beginning of a Jewish journey and a lifetime commitment to *tikkun olam* (repairing the world). 9 x 12, 32 pp, Full-color illus., HC, 978-1-58023-509-9 **$18.99** *For ages 3–6*

What You Will See Inside a Synagogue
By Rabbi Lawrence A. Hoffman, PhD, and Dr. Ron Wolfson; Full-color photos by Bill Aron
A colorful, fun-to-read introduction that explains the ways and whys of Jewish worship and religious life. 8½ x 10½, 32 pp, Full-color photos, Quality PB, 978-1-59473-256-0 **$8.99** *For ages 6 & up*
(A book from SkyLight Paths, Jewish Lights' sister imprint)

Because Nothing Looks Like God
By Lawrence Kushner and Karen Kushner
Real-life examples of happiness and sadness—from goodnight stories, to the hope and fear felt the first time at bat, to the closing moments of someone's life—invite parents and children to explore, together, the questions we all have about God, no matter what our age. 11 x 8½, 32 pp, Full-color illus., HC, 978-1-58023-092-6 **$17.99** *For ages 4 & up*

The Book of Miracles: A Young Person's Guide to Jewish Spiritual Awareness
Written and illus. by Lawrence Kushner
Easy-to-read, imaginatively illustrated book encourages kids' awareness of their own spirituality. Revealing the essence of Judaism in a language they can understand and enjoy. 6 x 9, 96 pp, 2-color illus., HC, 978-1-879045-78-1 **$16.95** *For ages 9–13*

In God's Hands   *By Lawrence Kushner and Gary Schmidt*
Brings new life to a traditional Jewish folktale, reminding parents and kids of all faiths and all backgrounds that each of us has the power to make the world a better place—working ordinary miracles with our everyday deeds. 9 x 12, 32 pp, Full-color illus., HC, 978-1-58023-224-1 **$16.99** *For ages 5 & up*

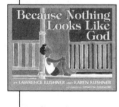

In Our Image: God's First Creatures
By Nancy Sohn Swartz
A playful new twist to the Genesis story, God asks all of nature to offer gifts to humankind—with a promise that the humans would care for creation in return. 9 x 12, 32 pp, Full-color illus., HC, 978-1-879045-99-6 **$16.95** *For ages 4 & up*

The Jewish Family Fun Book, 2nd Ed.
Holiday Projects, Everyday Activities, and Travel Ideas with Jewish Themes
By Danielle Dardashti and Roni Sarig
The complete sourcebook for families wanting to put a new spin on activities for Jewish holidays, holy days and the everyday. It offers dozens of easy-to-do activities that bring Jewish tradition to life for kids of all ages.
6 x 9, 304 pp, w/ 70+ b/w illus., Quality PB, 978-1-58023-333-0 **$18.99**

The Kids' Fun Book of Jewish Time   *By Emily Sper*
A unique way to introduce children to the Jewish calendar—night and day, the seven-day week, Shabbat, the Hebrew months, seasons and dates.
9 x 7½, 24 pp, Full-color illus., HC, 978-1-58023-311-8 **$16.99** *For ages 3–6*

What Makes Someone a Jew?   *By Lauren Seidman*
Reflects the changing face of American Judaism. Helps preschoolers and young readers (ages 3–6) understand that you don't have to look a certain way to be Jewish. 10 x 8½, 32 pp, Full-color photos, Quality PB, 978-1-58023-321-7 **$8.99** *For ages 3–6*

When a Grandparent Dies: A Kid's Own Remembering Workbook for
Dealing with Shiva and the Year Beyond   *By Nechama Liss-Levinson*
8 x 10, 48 pp, 2-color text, HC, 978-1-879045-44-6 **$15.95** *For ages 7–13*

Bar/Bat Mitzvah

The Mitzvah Project Book
Making Mitzvah Part of Your Bar/Bat Mitzvah ... and Your Life
By Liz Suneby and Diane Heiman; Foreword by Rabbi Jeffrey K. Salkin; Preface by Rabbi Sharon Brous
The go-to source for Jewish young adults and their families looking to make the
world a better place through good deeds—big or small.
6 x 9, 224 pp, Quality PB Original, 978-1-58023-458-0 **$16.99** For ages 11–13

The Bar/Bat Mitzvah Memory Book, 2nd Edition: An Album for Treasuring
the Spiritual Celebration
By Rabbi Jeffrey K. Salkin and Nina Salkin
8 x 10, 48 pp, 2-color text, Deluxe HC, ribbon marker, 978-1-58023-263-0 **$19.99**

For Kids—Putting God on Your Guest List, 2nd Edition: How to Claim the
Spiritual Meaning of Your Bar or Bat Mitzvah *By Rabbi Jeffrey K. Salkin*
6 x 9, 144 pp, Quality PB, 978-1-58023-308-8 **$15.99** For ages 11–13

The Jewish Prophet: Visionary Words from Moses and Miriam to Henrietta Szold
and A. J. Heschel *By Rabbi Dr. Michael J. Shire*
6½ x 8½, 128 pp, 123 full-color illus., HC, 978-1-58023-168-8 **$14.95**

Putting God on the Guest List, 3rd Edition: How to Reclaim the Spiritual
Meaning of Your Child's Bar or Bat Mitzvah *By Rabbi Jeffrey K. Salkin*
6 x 9, 224 pp, Quality PB, 978-1-58023-222-7 **$16.99**; HC, 978-1-58023-260-9 **$24.99**

Putting God on the Guest List Teacher's Guide
8½ x 11, 48 pp, PB, 978-1-58023-226-5 **$8.99**

Teens / Young Adults

Text Messages: A Torah Commentary for Teens
Edited by Rabbi Jeffrey K. Salkin
Shows today's teens how each Torah portion contains worlds of meaning for
them, for what they are going through in their lives, and how they can shape their
Jewish identity as they enter adulthood.
6 x 9, 304 pp (est), HC, 978-1-58023-507-5 **$24.99**

Hannah Senesh: Her Life and Diary, the First Complete Edition
By Hannah Senesh; Foreword by Marge Piercy; Preface by Eitan Senesh; Afterword by Roberta Grossman
6 x 9, 368 pp, b/w photos, Quality PB, 978-1-58023-342-2 **$19.99**

I Am Jewish: Personal Reflections Inspired by the Last Words of Daniel Pearl
Edited by Judea and Ruth Pearl 6 x 9, 304 pp, Deluxe PB w/ flaps, 978-1-58023-259-3 $18.99
Download a free copy of the *I Am Jewish Teacher's Guide* at www.jewishlights.com.

The JGirl's Guide: The Young Jewish Woman's Handbook for Coming of Age
By Penina Adelman, Ali Feldman and Shulamit Reinharz
6 x 9, 240 pp, Quality PB, 978-1-58023-215-9 **$14.99** For ages 11 & up

The JGirl's Teacher's and Parent's Guide
8½ x 11, 56 pp, PB, 978-1-58023-225-8 **$8.99**

Tough Questions Jews Ask, 2nd Edition: A Young Adult's Guide to Building a
Jewish Life *By Rabbi Edward Feinstein*
6 x 9, 160 pp, Quality PB, 978-1-58023-454-2 **$16.99** For ages 11 & up

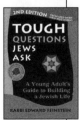

Tough Questions Jews Ask Teacher's Guide
8½ x 11, 72 pp, PB, 978-1-58023-187-9 **$8.95**

Pre-Teens

Be Like God: God's To-Do List for Kids
By Dr. Ron Wolfson
Encourages kids ages eight through twelve to use their God-given superpowers
to find the many ways they can make a difference in the lives of others and find
meaning and purpose for their own.
7 x 9, 144 pp, Quality PB, 978-1-58023-510-5 **$15.99** For ages 8–12

The Book of Miracles: A Young Person's Guide to Jewish Spiritual Awareness
By Lawrence Kushner, with all-new illustrations by the author.
6 x 9, 96 pp, 2-color illus., HC, 978-1-879045-78-1 **$16.95** For ages 9–13

About Jewish Lights

People of all faiths and backgrounds yearn for books that attract, engage, educate, and spiritually inspire.

Our principal goal is to stimulate thought and help all people learn about who the Jewish People are, where they come from, and what the future can be made to hold. While people of our diverse Jewish heritage are the primary audience, our books speak to people in the Christian world as well and will broaden their understanding of Judaism and the roots of their own faith.

We bring to you authors who are at the forefront of spiritual thought and experience. While each has something different to say, they all say it in a voice that you can hear.

Our books are designed to welcome you and then to engage, stimulate, and inspire. We judge our success not only by whether or not our books are beautiful and commercially successful, but by whether or not they make a difference in your life.

For your information and convenience, at the back of this book we have provided a list of other Jewish Lights books you might find interesting and useful. They cover all the categories of your life:

Bar/Bat Mitzvah	Life Cycle
Bible Study / Midrash	Meditation
Children's Books	Men's Interest
Congregation Resources	Parenting
Current Events / History	Prayer / Ritual / Sacred Practice
Ecology / Environment	Social Justice
Fiction: Mystery, Science Fiction	Spirituality
Grief / Healing	Theology / Philosophy
Holidays / Holy Days	Travel
Inspiration	Twelve Steps
Kabbalah / Mysticism / Enneagram	Women's Interest

Stuart M. Matlins, Publisher

Or phone, fax, mail or e-mail to: **JEWISH LIGHTS Publishing**
Sunset Farm Offices, Route 4 • P.O. Box 237 • Woodstock, Vermont 05091
Tel: (802) 457-4000 • Fax: (802) 457-4004 • www.jewishlights.com
Credit card orders: (800) 962-4544 (8:30AM–5:30PM EST Monday–Friday)
Generous discounts on quantity orders. SATISFACTION GUARANTEED. Prices subject to change.